How to be a Brilliant Mentor

How to be a Brilliant Mentor is an informal and accessible book that provides ideas and reassurance to help support you in your work as a teacher-training mentor. The authors are experienced trainers, teachers and mentors and bring together a wealth of expertise and research, offering clear and practical guidelines to enhance your mentoring, helping you to analyse your own practice and to understand the complex and often ambiguous role of the mentor in school.

Considering why you might become a mentor and what you can gain from the experience, *How to be a Brilliant Mentor* provides practical strategies and direct problem-solving to help you move promising trainees quickly beyond mere competence. It explores:

- collaborative working;
- giving effective feedback;
- emotional intelligence and developing and maintaining relationships;
- dealing with critical incidents;
- developing reflective practice;
- what to do if relationships break down;
- the relationship between coaching and mentoring;
- mentoring newly qualified teachers as well as trainees.

Covering a range of contexts, and dealing specifically with secondary and primary schools, it is illustrated with the experiences of real trainees, providing an insight into the surprising intensity of this relationship.

How to be a Brilliant Mentor can be dipped into for innovative mentoring ideas or read from cover to cover as a short, enjoyable course that will give you added confidence in your mentoring role.

The book is a companion to *How to be a Brilliant Trainee Teacher*, also by Trevor Wright.

Trevor Wright, University of Worcester, UK, has been a successful teacher for about thirty years, and a trainer of teachers for about fifteen years. His experiences as both teacher and teacher-trainer allow him to bridge the gap between principle and practice on a day-to-day basis.

Also by Trevor Wright:
How to be a Brilliant Teacher
How to be a Brilliant Trainee Teacher
How to be a Brilliant English Teacher

How to be a Brilliant Mentor

Developing outstanding teachers

Edited by
Trevor Wright

Routledge
Taylor & Francis Group

LONDON AND NEW YORK

First edition published 2010
by Routledge
2 Park Square, Milton Park, Abingdon, Oxon OX14 4RN

Simultaneously published in the USA and Canada
by Routledge
270 Madison Avenue, New York, NY 10016

Routledge is an imprint of the Taylor & Francis Group, an informa business

© 2010 selection and editorial material, Trevor Wright;
individual chapters, the contributors

Typeset in Sabon and Gill Sans by
Florence Production Ltd, Stoodleigh, Devon
Printed and bound in Great Britain by
TJ International Ltd, Padstow, Cornwall

British Library Cataloguing in Publication Data
A catalogue record for this book is available from the British Library

Library of Congress Cataloging-in-Publication Data
  How to be a brilliant mentor/edited by Trevor Wright. – 1st ed.
     p. cm.
  Includes bibliographical references and index.
  1. Mentoring in education.   2. Teachers – Training of.
  I. Wright, Trevor, 1950–
  LB1731.4.H68 2010
  371.102 – dc22   2009050240

ISBN13: 978–0–415–49213–3 (hbk)
ISBN13: 978–0–415–49214–0 (pbk)
ISBN13: 978–0–203–84993–4 (ebk)

Contents

Contributors

Paul Clarke has been a secondary teacher and examiner and is currently a senior lecturer within the Institute of Education at the University of Worcester. Publications include student books for GCSE business and citizenship and teacher books for business education and citizenship, and he has made a long-time contribution to the work of the Economic, Business and Enterprise Association.

Jacqueline Cuerden has taught at secondary level for twenty-two years. She has been a head of English, recently relinquishing the role in order to concentrate on her own research. She is a department mentor, and a subject moderator for the PGCE English programme at the University of Worcester, where she is also a mentor coach. Jacqueline has just completed a Master's degree in educational management and leadership, focusing her research on the induction process and the experiences of NQTs.

David Flint has been a teacher and examiner and is currently head of the Centre for Primary Initial Teacher Education at the University of Worcester. Publications include *EdExcel GCSE Geography Syllabus B Student Text*, together with numerous books on teaching primary geography. He also co-wrote the children's television series *Geography Starts Here!*

Shaun Hughes has been a secondary teacher, an advanced skills teacher and a partnership development advisor. He is currently a senior lecturer within the Institute of Education at the University of Worcester, where he leads on the Postgraduate Certificate in Mentoring and Coaching. Shaun has a background in the Arts and is interested in creative approaches to learning, teaching and research. He also works as a freelance illustrator.

Sandra Newell was a secondary teacher for nineteen years, then a senior lecturer in education at the University of Worcester for ten years. She is currently training to be a psychotherapist. She is co-author of the book *Behaviour Management in the Classroom: A Transactional Analysis Approach* (2002, David Fulton).

John Sears has recently retired as head of the Centre for Secondary Education at the University of Worcester. Prior to that, he taught science for twenty years in mixed comprehensives across the country, before embarking on a career as a teacher-trainer at Nottingham University and Canterbury Christchurch College. John also worked as a provider link adviser for the Training and Development Agency. He has authored several science textbooks and is co-editor of *Issues in Science Education*.

Alison Winson has been a secondary teacher and examiner and is currently a senior lecturer within the Institute of Education at the University of Worcester. Publications include *Revise for OCR GCSE: Food Technology* and contributions to books that have focused on teaching and learning within the area of secondary design and technology.

Sue Wood-Griffiths has been a design and technology teacher and head of department in schools in the UK, Germany and Thailand. She is currently a senior lecturer within the Institute of Education at the University of Worcester, contributing both to primary and secondary design and technology courses. Previous publications for Routledge include contributions to *A Practical Guide to Teaching Design and Technology in the Secondary School* and *Learning to Teach Design and Technology in the Secondary School*.

Trevor Wright has been a secondary teacher and examiner and is currently a senior lecturer within the Institute of Education at the University of Worcester. Publications include short stories for the BBC, two novels – *The Shifting Pier* (1989, Hamish Hamilton) and *Going Under* (1996, Gollancz) – and, for Routledge, *How to be a Brilliant English Teacher*, *How to be a Brilliant Trainee Teacher* and *How to be a Brilliant Teacher*.

Acknowledgements

Many trainees, university colleagues and school mentors have supported this book, and I should like to thank them all. In particular, the following trainee teachers (now qualified) have been active in the book's preparation: Cheryl Carrington, Laura Clark, Nicholas Cooke, Hannah Griffiths, Rachel Harper, Tom Hutton, Lydia Kenney, Keira Lapsley, Carly McHale, Beth Mikata, Becky Millward, Tom Mott, Claire Rowland, Kerry Stinton, Amanda Stone, Gail Thompson, Dominque Thrower and Stacy Wilson.

I should also like to thank Wendy Logan for the index and Shaun Hughes for the illustrations.

Chapter 1

The pivotal importance of the mentor

Trevor Wright

Mentoring is a crucial process. The training of teachers drives the quality of the education service, and the mentor is at the heart of that training. While other training components (such as the role of the university or school provider) vary according to the training scheme, the centrality of the mentor is a constant. She has a relationship with the trainee that no one else can equal, and her influence is the major determiner of the success, nature and quality of the new teacher.

We need to begin from this point because it's easy to underestimate this role. Historically, we have used the term *mentor* to describe the school-based teacher who will assume a supervisory responsibility for a trainee. Indeed, there are mentors who still regard the teaching placement as a sort of work experience, and the mentor's job as essentially one of practice oversight. Given the gradual spread of training models – the growth of school-based schemes, for example, such as the Graduate Teacher Programme, the proliferation of school-centred initial teacher training (SCITT) providers and the success of the Teach First initiative – we need to refocus on what mentors are doing. Theirs is arguably the single biggest contribution in establishing the quality of the teaching profession.

What mentoring isn't

Let's consider in more depth some of these limited notions of mentoring. As we've said, there is a not uncommon view that the trainee teacher is in school to 'practise', and that the mentor's job is to oversee this process, to offer advice where appropriate and, at some point, to assess performance. This notion of *practice* is confusing. The word itself means different things. Family doctors *practise* (in *practices*), but we hope that this doesn't mean they are learning on the job. Established teachers quite properly seek to extend and improve their own *practice*. The word has various, sometimes almost contradictory, meanings, and, when applied to trainee teachers in school, it's misleading.

It doesn't help that *practice* is often paired with its supposed opposite – *theory*. A sixth-former recently told me she'd passed her *theory* driving test. She said, 'So . . . I can drive now. In *theory*.' This was a joke: she meant that she couldn't drive at all, certainly not legally, until she passed the *practice* test as well. This pairing has a clear attitudinal hierarchy: theory is all very well, but it's practice that really matters. It's an unhelpful separation, which is compounded if we see school practice in such terms. It's a common enough notion among trainees and mentors. We learn the theory at university, then the real stuff at school. Quite often, we struggle to see the connections. Quite often, we resent the theory as a necessary evil. Graduate trainee applicants at interview often explain that they have chosen this route because they want to get on with the job and not be held back by theory. This division is demeaning to the teaching profession and to all aspects of the training. Theory matters, and, in any case, just as university isn't just about theory, school placements aren't, and mustn't be, just about practice.

Let's begin, then, with a clear definition. Trainee teachers don't come to your school to practise. They don't come for work experience or even job sampling. Of course, they will do all of these things, but there is one single purpose behind them. They are with you to *train*.

New mentors, undergoing their own training, will often ask about what the trainees have to do. A teacher does many things during the day that go well beyond planning, teaching and marking. She does break duties. She covers for sick colleagues. She invigilates. She attends many meetings. In discussing which of these activities are suitable for trainees, new mentors often begin from the premise that, in fact, they should do *all* of them. *Teachers do these things, so trainees should do them too.*

There's certainly some logic here. Trainees need to see the whole of the job, and we need to see that they can manage it. I remember being almost overwhelmed by the aspects of my first teaching post that no one had prepared me for. This was a long time ago, and I remember being bewildered (for example) by collecting dinner

money. But, nevertheless, this is a limited logic because it grossly underestimates the *training* function of the placement and of the mentor.

Let's replace the mantra, 'Teachers do it, so trainees should do it too', with the question, 'To what extent is it a *training* activity?'. You could begin by listing the many activities that you, as a teacher, are involved in every day. They would include planning, assessing, administrating, teaching, conversing, meeting, supervising. The teacher's brief is a wide one, and this is a varied list. But next you need to look at each activity and consider its training potential. Is completing a corridor duty really a rich *training* opportunity?

Such a straightforward audit of the teacher's job in terms of training potential may well result in the immediate removal of some activities from the trainee's programme. I managed to do break duties for several decades, and my exam invigilation was refined and artful, but nobody ever trained me in these things. If the training potential is so limited, then they shouldn't be doing them. Your trainee probably has one year to qualify, and in that very short time her priorities must focus on teaching and learning.

Beyond simply striking out some of these day-to-day activities, you might, by applying the big question, modify some of the rest, so that they become authentic training components. A tearful trainee phoned me recently to discuss her workload. Her mentor, working on the 'teachers have to do it' premise, had given her one hundred Year 9 examination papers to mark. This was a fairly insensitive notion on a number of counts, including (of course) a spectacular forgetfulness about the pressures a trainee is under. Sometimes, there seems to be almost an element of machismo in such requests. The trainee herself suspected that the mentor was offloading his own work onto her, and this (whether true or not) was not helping their working relationship. But what worried me most was that the mentor was not considering the *training* potential of the activity.

The trainee will learn something from marking one hundred scripts, but it won't be very much or very reliable. She will learn something about teachers' workload, but even that will be compromised, because what may look like a tiresome prospect to an experienced professional looks suicidally impossible to a trainee. (Most mainstream activities, such as marking or lesson planning, can take a trainee between five and ten times as long as a regular teacher.) So even the fairly minimal understanding of a teacher's job offered by such a task is bound to be wildly inaccurate.

More to the point, the sheer volume of work here is virtually guaranteed to minimise any new learning about assessment practice. In another school, I observed a simple piece of collaborative working between a mentor and a trainee. They were co-marking a piece of GCSE course work. The mentor led the conversation. They had the script and the assessment criteria in front of them, and I listened as the mentor explained how she was applying the criteria, interpreting them in practical terms as she read the child's work. In fact, this was a piece of constructivist teaching. The trainee was increasingly encouraged to join in, to offer her judgements, to make sense of the grade definitions through the examples in front of her. They turned to a second script. This time, the trainee led the conversation.

This is a simple idea, and we will talk more about collaborative working in later chapters. It was extraordinarily exciting to watch, as the school context, with real children and real assessment, moved the trainee so quickly towards confidence and, indeed, competence. She went on to assess more scripts, on her own. How many scripts are necessary to furnish real training in this way? What matters is the collaboration, the scaffolding, the application. If she could now mark and then rediscuss six or ten more scripts, she would be genuinely learning about assessment. This may not be what teachers do every day. They don't have time for such collaborations; they have one hundred scripts to mark. But it's what trainees need.

This may be an extreme example, but I offer it to clarify the difference between these two mentoring attitudes. They are opposite in kind, not just in degree. The first approach, based on simple job sampling, is almost designed to destroy confidence; the second – based on training – is focused and developmental and has clear outcomes. It validates and dignifies the role of the mentor as a centrally placed teacher-trainer.

What we are saying is that a teaching placement is not an apprenticeship. Of course, the trainee will work closely with you, as a trainee plumber works alongside a professional; she will watch, emulate and learn, but this will be only a small part of her activity and of her relationship with you. It is far from central. Of course, you are an experienced and expert teacher – indeed, you are expanding this experience through your mentoring. You know how to run a classroom; you have much to demonstrate and to offer your trainee. It's not uncommon for trainees, impressed and encouraged by their mentors, to become increasingly frustrated as they try to behave like them in the classroom. They need to watch, they need to understand why you do what you do, but this doesn't mean that they need to copy. Mentoring isn't a masterclass. It's a complex range of training activities, and this makes for a complex relationship. This relationship between input and output is discussed in more detail in the next chapter.

We are making some preliminary suggestions here as to the criteria lying behind these activities. We have already said that trainees don't necessarily have to do everything that a teacher does, because some of those things don't offer serious training potential. Second, we have said that the activities that are properly enlisted as training activities – such as assessment tasks – need to be focused and useful. For example, they probably need a strong collaborative content. Third, of course, we should add that a training programme will need to feature activities that teachers don't normally engage with, or at least not explicitly. Teachers probably don't write assignments, or maintain audits of subject knowledge; possibly, they don't even plan lessons in the way that trainees have to. They perhaps don't attend regular, school-based training sessions on local and national policies. Trainees need to do all of these things, and the mentor is a key figure in creating and monitoring such activity.

Partnership

Successful mentoring depends absolutely on the notion of partnership, and this means that the mentor has to understand, shape and support the full range of training components. It's not unusual for mentors to subscribe to the 'theory and practice' fallacy. For the best of reasons, they may welcome trainees into their schools and try to reassure them that the formidable academic demands of the training are less important than success in the classroom. The provider may insist on various planning protocols: for example, it may insist that lessons are planned always from learning objectives, rather than from activities. Or it may insist that lessons, once taught, are formally evaluated, in writing. Genuinely overwhelmed by the workload, as trainees often are, the trainee turns to the mentor for solace. Genuinely concerned to help, he may advise her that some, or all, of these demands aren't important. He is an excellent teacher, and he hasn't planned or evaluated a lesson for six years. 'Stop worrying; it's your classroom performance that counts. This is the false division between the airy-fairy world of university and the nitty-gritty of reality in schools.'

Such fragmentation, however kindly it's intended, is ultimately and fundamentally detrimental to the training. It does the trainee no favours. She has to work to make a coherence out of her training, and the mentor has to help. This is one of the flaws of the apprenticeship model. The mentor (as we've said) is experienced and expert; and here we have a paradox. The more experienced and expert we become, the less we need to think explicitly and analytically about what we're doing. The age-old analogy of learning to drive is apposite here. Good drivers steer, react, change gear without a single conscious thought, and, in fact, it's quite difficult to explain to a learner exactly how to use the clutch. The expert teacher probably operates at a high level of skilled pragmatism, and this is a considerable achievement. She probably doesn't discuss learning theory in the staffroom; she does very well without it. But a trainee trying to emulate skilled pragmatism is bound to fail, because she has neither the skill nor the experience to allow this to happen. The trainee's pragmatism is unskilled because it's uninformed. The skilled mentor has to be much more than a skilled teacher: she is a skilled teacher who has understood the need to deconstruct her own practice in order that the trainee can join her in an explicit understanding of it. This understanding then becomes one of a range of significant inputs for the trainee that she has to reconcile and make sense of as she builds her own practice.

Defragmentation

Fragmentation is one of the problems that beset trainees. They receive conflicting advice. They face conflicting demands. At one minute, they're trying to get Jasmine to stop swearing at them; at the next, they're reading Bruner on constructivism. We know, as experienced teachers, that this range of inputs simply reflects the richness and diversity of teaching, but trainees need more help than this. They have to reconcile, to defragment their experience. The mentor's job is to help with this process. She needs to sit at the centre, not at one end. She needs to help the trainee to join the airy-fairy to the nitty-gritty. After all, Bruner may have something to say about Jasmine.

To do this, the mentor must understand and indeed influence the training partnership. If you disagree with some of the emphases of the training – if, for example, you think that some of the demands of the university provider are irrelevant or unrealistic – you need to deal with that at an appropriate level. You need to become involved with this at the planning stage. These are structural, strategic discussions about the nature of the training, and the trainee should not be directly involved in them.

I work with a number of SCITT organisations. Coming from a university-provider background, I approached my first SCITT with some suspicion. I expected to discover a pragmatic training model,

a process based almost wholly on nitty-gritty, with only lip service paid to airy-fairy. It's certainly true that SCITTs have to work very hard at areas that aren't systemically natural to them, such as learning theory, or the building of subject knowledge, while, on the other hand, they are especially effective with issues such as behaviour management. This is hardly surprising; research under-lines this, and it's common sense, anyway. But what I have found to be unexpectedly successful is the sense of partnership within an SCITT. Traditionally, university providers work within partner-ships. In practice, these partnerships are pyramidal. Mentors are involved: they attend planning and maintenance meetings, but it's structurally inevitable that the university runs the partnership. It's in such systems that fragmentation may occur. A great strength of the SCITT, on the other hand, is that its members are its staff. There may be one or two SCITT tutors, but most of the training, whether handled centrally or in schools, is carried out by mentors. Teachers in SCITTs don't feel themselves to be junior part-ners; indeed, in a strong SCITT, they aren't partners at all. They *are* the organisation. The trainees' confidence is high because they see consistency of value and approach wherever they look. *In any organisation, the brilliant mentor is one who identifies with the whole of the training.*

The mentor must help the trainee to make sense of her potentially fractured experiences, so that she can defragment and synthesise her inputs into coherent outcomes. Triangulation is an asset here.

A common problem is the difficulty of drawing together the range of conversations that might take place around any single training issue. The mentor feels, for example, that the trainee is making little progress. A number of discussions will be had: the mentor will talk to the trainee; the trainee may talk to her tutor; the mentor and the tutor will talk together. There may be other people involved as well. Several conversations will happen, over a period of time; they will cover the same ground, but with a range of nuances that reflect various relationships and aspirations. A conversation will report and interpret other conversations. Misunderstandings and inconsistencies will arise that will themselves deter progress. Well-intentioned suggestions are seen as insensitive criticisms; sincere explanations become defensive excuses; careful reassurances are taken as partiality. It can become impossible to disentangle these confusions and to rebuild a rational narrative about what's happen-ing and what needs to be done.

Of the three individuals usually concerned, any one can, at any time, find himself trying to make sense of this kind of muddle. I have found myself in the middle of it on many occasions. Versions of the issues have become polarised and irreconcilable. Two completely different accounts of the problem are presented; blame is apportioned variously. The trainee admits to arriving late for one meeting; the mentor has a list of meetings missed and other unprofessional behaviour. In trying to mediate, I later find that my own remarks have been recast differently by both parties.

This is human nature, a mixture of family argument and office politics. Throughout this book, we will offer many suggestions of protocols that should reduce these tensions, but it's worth mentioning triangulation at the outset. My own inclination initially was to speak separately to the parties, to move from one to the other, as I believe Henry Kissinger did, with questionable success, in the 1960s. I have learned that lasting resolutions happen when all parties sit together with a clear agenda and actually talk about relationships as well as pedagogy. This can be challenging and also difficult to organise, but it's the only way, finally, to reach agreed positions and to move forward. Some providers actually produce their final assessment grades for each trainee – at the end of the course – in triangulated meetings with trainee, mentor and tutor.

Behaviour

Let's consider behaviour management as an example of a mentoring focus. This has implications for the depth of activity, as well as the range.

The first thing to say is that behaviour management mustn't be allowed to dominate your work with your trainee. It can easily do so, for good and obvious reasons. Behaviour concerns new trainees more than any other aspect of the work. It's what they worry about before and after starting their training. Quite properly, it also concerns mentors: if the children don't listen, then good planning and ingenious resources are of no account. Initial feedback sessions are frequently based on these precepts, and it's common for no other issues to be involved at all. Until we can get the behaviour right, nothing else is worth considering, because nothing else will work.

Further, the mentor will embrace behaviour management because it's work that clearly belongs to the school. The central (university) training will provide discussion, video, theory, but the school has the real thing – naughty children in actual lessons – and the trainee has to face up to this on a practical, day-to-day basis. All of this makes good sense, but we need to remember that our criterion for activity is the training criterion. The trainee needs help in transforming pragmatic survival tactics into genuine, strategic understanding.

First, then, you should as mentor resist the temptation to focus solely on children's behaviour, even at the outset. Second, your work on behaviour needs to move beyond the pragmatic.

Discussions with trainees often focus on two areas. The most common is the school's sanctions-and-rewards policy. Many schools have elaborate systems, and of course trainees, like new staff members, need to understand and to use them. Often, a piece of lesson feedback will note the misapplication of such a policy and recommend its better use in solving the trainee's problem.

Of course, the proper use of such policies is essential. They build trainees' confidence because, however they work in detail, they are a constant reassurance that the teacher isn't alone in the classroom. The very existence of these systems reminds everyone involved – including children – that good and bad behaviour aren't simply functions of personal relationship. Indeed, a behaviour policy is effective because it depersonalises behaviour. Against such a policy background, bad behaviour is a challenge and an affront, not to the trainee (or the individual teacher) but to the school. If you behave badly, you are offending the institution, and the institution will deal with it. This can place the teacher in a powerful position, where poor behaviour isn't a personal failure but a choice made by a pupil in respect of his attitude to the whole school. These ideas are strongly reassuring to trainees, but they need to be discussed at this level of explicit analysis before they begin to have lasting effects in building their confidence. This is a move through pragmatism to reflection and principle.

The second area often brought up by mentors is the set of personal and professional qualities loosely known as management skills. The mentor may discuss voice, presence, pace, confidence. He may talk about low-key, non-confrontational relationships. All of this is worth discussion, but mentors must remember the point of feedback. *Feedback* isn't, in fact, a particularly useful term, because it suggests looking backwards, when actually the point of the post-lesson discussion is to look forwards; and so comments on teacher performance need to be associated with mechanisms for improvement. In fact, feedback is one part of the process of analysis and reflection that drives the progress of every trainee. We will return to this in later chapters.

These two areas – school policy and teacher skills – are usually the only contexts in which behaviour is discussed. They are, in a sense, both concerned with what is sometimes known as *extrinsic* behaviour management, and a mentor who sees himself as nitty-gritty practitioner may be satisfied with this coverage. Extrinsic work will certainly get you through some school-based difficulties and effect some classroom improvement, but, for feedback to be truly developmental, it needs to cover more complex and analytical areas where the trainee can discover transferable skills. I have no doubt that real progress is made in behaviour when the trainee considers the deeper and more lasting significance of *intrinsic* learning management.

Intrinsic management works from the principle that behaviour is best enhanced through the work. Good lesson planning will often deliver the right pupil response; or, to put it the other way, bad planning will certainly generate bad behaviour. Good planning in this sense includes, for example, clarity of learning objectives; differentiation of activities; the sensible deployment of variety and choice; the pitching of work at the right level; the intelligent design of resources; the careful preparation of teacher explanation and task-setting; the planning of lessons with clear throughlines and well thought-out transitions.

For example, a common and current syndrome within lesson planning, which leads straight to bad behaviour (as well as poor learning), sometimes stems from a preoccupation with *interactivity*. Recent UK strategies have emphasised the importance of this, and of course it's to be welcomed. We want children to be more involved in their lessons and their learning. We want to recognise that they are sometimes experts, and that certainly they bring opinions and experiences to the classroom. We don't want the teacher to stand at the front and lecture. These developments and attitudes offer improvements in terms of learning and, indeed, of behaviour. But the term *interactive* is in danger of being overused and misunderstood.

Consistent with this belief in interactivity, these strategies posit a planning attitude that is based largely on pupil activity. Lesson-planning formats almost always consist of blank spaces where the teacher must indicate what the pupils will do. This may well be a radical and welcome development from planning a decade ago, which, if it existed at all, probably consisted of teacher-notes concerning the content of the lesson. In other words, we've swung from planning teacher activity to planning pupil activity.

Trainees embrace this planning approach and produce lively, engaging lessons as a result. But there's a tacit diffidence growing up around this, and a common problem in the classrooms of new teachers stems from their unwillingness to plan *themselves* into their lessons. Of course we don't want them to stand at the front and just talk, but they do need to understand the difference between teaching a lesson and administrating it. Many trainees will work very hard at preparing pupil activity. They will produce excellent, progressive and attractive materials. But all too often, in the classroom, they seem to believe that the carefully made worksheets will carry the lesson. Their job is to make the worksheets beforehand and then to distribute them and settle the children to them. Little or no explanation is offered regarding the ideas, the concepts being explored. Teacher talk is limited to fairly brisk task-setting. As a result, the children find that they don't know what to do. They can't complete the worksheets, because they don't understand the ideas behind them. When discussing this afterwards, the trainee will say, 'Well . . . I didn't want to dominate. I wanted it to come from them . . .'. This is honest and sound intuition, but a balance must be struck. Teachers shouldn't lecture but they shouldn't be afraid to teach. Discovery is great, but explorers need guides as well as maps.

This is the beginning of a detailed and complex discussion about how pupil behaviour is affected by the work of the lesson, by its manner and content, by the planning. Children who don't understand will become disenchanted; they will stray off task; they will become uninterested and distracted. When she analyses this with her trainee, the mentor needs to move beyond rewards and sanctions; she needs to move beyond teacher performance. She needs, in fact, to move beyond the pragmatic and into a wide and deep conversation that ranges over many aspects of teaching and learning, making connections for the trainee that are less obvious, more challenging and more yielding of long-term understanding. After this discussion, the trainee needs to look again at her planning. She perhaps needs to plan her *transitions* more fully, thinking in advance about the language she will use in lifting the lesson from one activity to the next. She is looking forwards, not back, and she is working strategically as well as tactically.

Learning objectives

Let's look at another example of how the mentor needs to position himself centrally, to analyse his own practice and help the trainee to synthesise inputs. This relates to learning objectives. I taught for about thirty years without thinking much about them. Indeed, I was fairly suspicious of the whole idea, seeing myself as a creative teacher and my lessons as exploratory and unpredictable. Even today, when I attend training events that begin with the solemn 'PowerPointing' of the day's objectives, I feel a mixture of rage and despair. I know that, in six hours' time, I will be marched back into the hall and told that I've met them.

As a mentor, I probably communicated this attitude. I was a successful teacher; I didn't think about learning objectives; I planned lively and engaging activities without them. Any trainee or young teacher who came my way was so advised. I was a nitty-gritty mentor. It was only after several years of teacher training, with all of the opportunities for observation and reflection that go with that other job, that I began to see the point. I would watch trainees, who had given careful thought to their activities, teaching lively lessons, and I would wonder why those lessons went nowhere. It became clear to me that activities are fine, but they have to proceed from a sense of what pupils will know, understand or be able to do as a result of them. Pupils walk into the room and, an hour later, they must walk out with something they didn't walk in with. With my trainees, I call this the 0–60 rule. The lesson needs to be planned with a clear sense of what this will be. I picture it now, even after all these years, as a small, valuable, solid object. In fact, that's why I prefer the term learning *objective* to, for example, *intended learning outcome*. I came to see that apparently lively lessons actually lacked purpose, point and progression, when the basis of the planning was what children were going to *do*, not what they were going to *learn*. I have no doubt at all that trainees who understand learning objectives will prosper, and that those who don't, won't.

What the mentor has to do is to reconcile these issues, first for himself, and then for his trainee. We have here two opposing attitudes – that objectives are pointless, bureaucratic, arbitrary; and that they are essential. A trainee may find herself caught between these two views. Typically, the first view may belong to the school mentor, and the other to the central training provider. They appear to be a simple contradiction. What is the trainee to do about this? And how is the mentor going to help?

The nitty-gritty mentor positions himself at the practical, school end of the spectrum. His advice is that objectives are just a hoop to jump through, an airy-fairy construct of the theorists who run the universities and who haven't taught in a school for years, if ever, and to whom he sees himself as a necessary counterbalance. He does very well without them, and the trainee will be well advised to learn from his practice, and to stop worrying.

This is an understandable position; it's cheerful, practical and robust, and in the short term it seems to solve the problem. But, as a solution, it can't last: the demand for learning objectives still exists within the training, and the trainee will not progress without them. How can this be? How can they matter so much for the trainee and not at all for the mentor?

I realise that these are attitudinal stereotypes that may annoy either teachers or university lecturers, but I have to say that this sort of dilemma isn't uncommon. I have had variations of this conversation with many trainees. A typical pattern is that the trainee becomes absorbed into the school; on a long placement, she works to the mentor's pattern, and all seems to be well for a time. But then progress falters; there is a plateau (these things are well documented) or even a falling back. The early promise is dissipated; children are bored; they aren't learning. This is when the trainee needs to reconnect to the full range of the training, and the mentor must help her.

To do this, he must examine his own practice. The good mentor models it and explains it, but the brilliant mentor analyses it *for himself*. This is a two-stage process: *the mentor must think about what he himself does, and why he does it, before proceeding to work with the trainee.*

I have had such discussions with mentors several times. In this case, it's fairly simple. The mentor is a successful teacher, and this must surely mean that children are learning. Does he know *what* they're learning? Does he plan for this? Are his lively activities merely random, or do they have a point? Very possibly, he has become so expert in his work that he no longer needs to think about these things. He knows what activity delivers what learning, he knows why he's doing it – these things are second nature; activity and learning have become synonymous for him. The initial stage of planning – the learning objectives – is taken as read.

A simple self-analysis reminds the mentor about his own practice. Of course learning objectives lie at the heart of his classroom, though he long ago stopped calling them that, or thinking explicitly about them at all. Having worked this out, he is now in a position to move forward with the trainee in this vital area.

I have offered these two examples – of learning management and of learning objectives – as case studies illustrating the fundamentally important business of the positioning of the mentor. The good mentor puts himself at one end of the training continuum, but the brilliant mentor stands in the middle and accepts full responsibility as a teacher-trainer. We have also come to a second important principle, and this has to do with explicitness. It's vital that mentors understand the differences that experience makes. Even a few months of experience put teachers in quite different places compared with trainees, and it's easy to forget this. As you become more expert, you become more and more implicit and instinctual in your practice. This is inevitable and necessary. But a trainee needs explicitness. She needs more than just successful models – she isn't aiming to become you: she needs analysis, reflection and consequent understanding. This is perhaps the first switch you have to make when you become a mentor. You have to step back from your own work and look explicitly at it. Before you can fully support your trainee, you have to rediscover yourself.

Chapter 2

Inputs and outputs

Trevor Wright

In the first chapter, we discussed the positioning of the mentor as the pivotal centre of the training, and now it's time to consider some of the implications of this for the mentoring relationship. From the trainee's point of view, nothing is more important than this relationship, and he may spend more time than you imagine worrying about the impression he's making on you.

It's a complex relationship for a number of reasons. Your trainee is part pupil and part colleague. He is not a child, but he is certainly vulnerable. Your view of his ability will affect his life. Of course, like all teaching relationships, it's at least binary, in that you are supporting and developing but also assessing. Teachers are well used to the ambiguity of formative assessment, but this is peculiarly sensitive and potentially distorting when it involves an adult and a career. At times, your trainee may well feel that he's involved in a protracted reality-television interview show, in which you may be variously cast as Alan Sugar or Donald Trump.

It's obvious that this power can be an impediment. A common syndrome involves the trainee who doesn't want to admit to difficulties. Year 8 is getting worse by the day, but he's determined that he has to deal with this on his own. The fact that you, his first call for support, are also one of his judges, is bound to confuse the issue. It's a fatal confusion, because things will simply deteriorate up to the point where you have to step in anyway, and he has lost control in more ways than one. He may even realise this, but he still doesn't know what to do about it.

This inhibition may affect you as well as your trainee. I quite often receive expressions of concern from mentors about trainees. They will list the issues of practice and professionalism that are going wrong. I usually ask the mentor if she has spoken directly to the trainee in these terms. Commonly, she will reply that she has kept them to herself; she doesn't want to destroy the trainee's confidence.

This is a natural, generous and teacherly attitude but, more often than not, it's an unsuccessful approach. Simply waiting, hoping for things to get better, is rarely effective. Of course, confidence matters very much, but somehow the mentor must reconcile this with the need to be clear and explicit with the trainee.

Be explicit!

This *explicitness* is vital. We'll take an extreme example – of a trainee who is doing so badly that he becomes a formal cause for concern. In such a case, he will be notified in writing that things are not as they should be. He is provided with a set of targets, deadlines and accompanying support. All training routes have such procedures, and they are used only in serious cases where we might not be hopeful of success; but often we are wrong. Surprisingly, the trainee's fortunes may be reversed at this point, and he may go on to complete the training. In many cases, this is because the formal support procedure was the beginning of an explicit dialogue about his progress. If he's lucky, that dialogue isn't too late, but it really needed to start pre-emptively, and much earlier.

So, we have to be explicit without ruining confidence. What we need is a clear, professional context for these dialogues. Things will go wrong for trainees; this is a given. Learning to be a teacher is infinitely complex, contradictory and exhausting; frustrations and failures are inevitable along the way. We must begin from that shared understanding. Certainly, we are required to make judgements, but we should clarify at the outset how those judgements work. We expect things to go wrong; something going wrong isn't of itself a personal failure. We don't judge professional competence on that. What we judge on is what happens next. What does the trainee do about the problem? If he consistently fails to seek help, or is consistently defensive against help when it's offered, then he is not functioning professionally. If we have to judge, then that's where we do it. We don't judge on the problem; we judge on the resolution.

We need, then, to build a confident relationship that can contain explicit criticism. One contributor to this is positivity. This may seem so obvious as to be hardly worth mentioning, but it's extraordinary how habitually negative we can appear to be in professional dialogue – for example, in the giving of post-lesson feedback. I'm talking here, not about our *intentions* at such times, which are bound to be honourable and positive, but rather about how these conversations are *perceived* by our trainees. However we brand them – as developmental objectives, areas for consideration or progress pointers – our trainees see them as criticisms.

So, intention and perception may be poles apart, and this is where we need to start. We need to be explicit about the intention of a conversation. For example, we need to clarify whether we're offering supportive, developmental advice (a normal situation), or expressing genuine concerns (less normal). We may think that this is obvious, or alternatively that these things can't be separated, but our trainees need us to clarify as far as we can. They have no experience or perspective. For example, it's very common for lesson feedback to seem almost entirely negative. There's an 80/20 rule here: if our feedback isn't 80 per cent positive, it will feel 80 per cent negative to our trainees. If you think that that's an overprotective plea on behalf of oversensitive individuals, then I invite you to remember for yourself how it feels to be criticised, and I ask you to consider the low relative status of your trainee in these conversations.

I've done this myself. I gave detailed and developmental feedback to my very first trainee teacher. I went painstakingly through the lesson and offered many suggestions as to how it could have been improved. I was a young, creative and successful teacher and I wanted to pass on as much as I could to her. I assumed that she would go home thanking her lucky stars that she had come across me at this time. What she did in fact was to complain about me to her university.

The perceived negativity of feedback can be mitigated in various ways. Simply explaining your developmental intentions helps. Deliberately balancing the negative/positive ratio matters. Setting detailed criticism within an explicit context of approval helps ('I'm making this point because I've no doubt that you're going to do very well . . .'). You must also discipline yourself to involve the trainee's own views of the lesson – perhaps by asking for them as your opening gambit. And you must be sure to regulate your feedback, so that there are always compliments, and criticisms are few and focused.

This last is a key point, of course; you know this as a teacher. It goes beyond morale. A trainee needs a quantity of input that she can process and work on. Correcting every error is pointless. She needs focused targets and support. We will consider these later in this chapter as part of the reflective process.

The value of explicitness in the mentoring conversation can hardly be overestimated, and this may present difficulties because, as teachers, we aren't used to it. We are used to dealing with children; we are skilled in developing and enhancing working relationships through subtext, through the subliminal, through veiled threats, finessing and cajoling. It comes as a surprise that we can and should talk directly to trainees about themselves, their practice and their responses.

For example, a very common issue with trainees is defensiveness. A typical conversation may include this kind of exchange:

Mentor: You didn't really spend enough time explaining the ideas behind that task.
Trainee: Well, I didn't want to talk at them for too long . . .

Or. . .

Mentor: Your questioning would be better if you asked a range of question types.
Trainee: Yes, but I particularly needed to ask factual questions because I had to check their learning . . .

Such responses are understandable. In fact, to some extent, they're inevitable. The trainee has reasons for what he does and wants to justify himself. But repeated defences of this type, as well as being irritating, are a barrier to progress, because they evade development. In fact, openness to advice may well be the single biggest success indicator on a training course.

This matters, and so a mentor may say to me in private, 'He's very defensive. I do try. I try to put it in different ways. I try to compliment him as well. But he just can't take criticism.' I suggest to the mentor that she has reached a point where she needs to say this to the trainee, directly. She needs to say to him, 'Taking criticism is important to your progress. I don't think you're very good at it.' Mentors can be quite shocked at this suggestion, but the trainee can't really move forward in this or any area if no one will point it out to him. You need to have a dialogue about the dialogue. Of course, trainees react in different ways. Some will not be pleased – they will be defensive about being defensive – but many will think again. Even the ones who appear to dismiss your comments may go away and reflect privately on them. Perhaps they hadn't noticed that they were doing it, or they hadn't appreciated how significant it was. Tell them, directly. Tell them kindly but clearly what they're doing and why it matters. They aren't children.

What goes in and what comes out

What we are considering is the relationship between the trainee and her many training experiences. This is not a simple relationship based on emulation; such a view is bound to fail. In this simplistic version of the process, the trainee receives inputs and tries to copy them. The input may be her observation of you or another colleague; it may be a piece of reading or advice about behaviour management. It seems useful, or successful, and so the trainee attempts to replicate it in her practice. This simple input–output model may appear to work for a time, but it will inevitably collapse.

There are a number of reasons for this failure. One is that the trainee has to find her own practice, and this will be unique to her, just as yours is to you. Copying others may be useful or essential scaffolding activity, but, like all scaffolds, it is temporary. In fact, trainees often begin their training with clear, aspirational models of themselves as teachers. These models derive from various sources: the most common are based on the Hollywood-teacher model, the my-best-teacher model or a combination of the two.

The Hollywood teacher is dynamic and attractive. He is mould-breaking; he has an instinctive understanding of the pupils and makes astonishingly effective relationships, especially with the least promising of them. His colleagues resent and envy him in equal measure. He is unconventional. Above all, he is charismatic. This is an idealistic stimulus for a beginner, and there's nothing wrong with idealism, but the notion of teaching as dynamic performance is (of course) wrong-headed and ultimately harmful. Among other things, it excludes the pupils, except as awe-struck audience, and soon becomes a barrier to progress, because it focuses on teaching rather than learning.

Alternatively, many trainees start with a self-image based on their own favourite teachers. It's not unusual for them to begin their practice with a ready-made set of teacher mannerisms, often based on lively, whole-class questioning, that they have imported from their own happy schooldays. The image has to be reworked during the training, and trainees make good progress when they understand this process – when they understand, not only that they have to move beyond this initial replication mode, but why trying to be somebody else won't work for them. They are different people in different circumstances, and sometimes their pupils aren't as keen as they were when they were sitting in their own favourite lessons. Pupils instinctively spot and dislike fakery; the trainee has to find a teacher-version of herself that proceeds authentically from inside, not outside.

These initial input–output models need to be discussed, because the trainee learns important lessons from them. Most significantly, she learns that teaching is a complicated business, and that simple replication isn't enough; and this lesson needs to be reapplied to the many new inputs that will form the training. The mentor needs to work with the trainee to establish an input–output process that is functional and sophisticated.

What do we mean by *reflection*?

Inputs need to be digested when they arrive and before they can be used; this is a process of *reflection*. It's a term commonly used around teacher training; for example, trainees have to become *reflective practitioners* and, to help them with this, they will have to do *reflective writing*. The word itself isn't particularly helpful. For one thing, it may remind us of a mirror. In this association, reflection is replication, and in fact I'm offering reflection here as the essential process that takes us well beyond that. There's also something passive about the word: we might picture personal reflection as a sort of private, silent staring into space, a sort of mulling-over of things. It might contain elements of this, but if your trainee is to make sense of her experiences, reflection has to become a systematic, shared, active and targeted process. We could call this *dynamic reflection*.

A central component of this reflection is *synthesis*. In the previous chapter, we talked about the need to defragment the trainee's experience, to help her to resolve apparent contradictions. The trainee has to draw the inputs together and make sense of them. For example, she will be given conflicting advice. One teacher will tell her never to talk while children are talking – always demand and wait for silence; another colleague will point out that some lessons would never get started at all if such advice were followed. The trainee is confused. Which is the right way? To whom should she listen?

Of course, if she only received one piece of advice, there would be no confusion; but there would be little stimulus for reflection. The discussion of the *two* pieces of advice takes her towards an understanding of the complexity of teaching. In this sense, trainees need multiple inputs. To take another example, you might decide that a trainee's lesson beginnings are failing. The lessons start raggedly, and, as we all know, good beginnings are crucial. This judgement would be made, perhaps, during your observation of your trainee's teaching and would begin a process of dynamic reflection.

Among other reflective activities, you might decide that your trainee needs to watch some effective lesson openings. If she only observes *one* effective teacher managing *one* effective lesson beginning, she has little ground for reflection and synthesis, however impressive the exemplar may be. She can attempt to replicate it. If it works, it will help pragmatically with the overcoming of a problem, but the trainee is unlikely to understand why it's effective and so won't be able to adapt or reapply it. The old adage about charitable aid works well here: your trainee doesn't need food; she needs the understanding that will help her to grow her own food. And, of course, if the simple replication doesn't work for her, without reflection the whole process may have been a waste of time.

Some simple rules apply here. This is not random activity, but a *focused*, thematic programme. The activity is pointless if it isn't *targeted* (on a development area for the trainee) and if it doesn't yield material for *reflection*. It may even be destructive. Furthermore, your trainee needs *plurality*. You need to find two or more colleagues who begin their lessons effectively but differently. Finally, you must create opportunities for discussion and comparison – either with yourself or with the observed teachers. *Reflection begins with discussion.*

In summary, we are saying that the input–output model for trainees must be complex if it is to be effective. A simple input–output model is based on replication. Good practice is observed and copied. This is a two-stage process in which the trainee herself is almost non-existent. It can have no long- or medium-term benefit; if it works in the short term, it is a matter of good fortune. The complex model, a three-stage process, places dynamic reflection between the input and the output. Discussion, synthesis, comparison, contrast, selection and personal evaluation transform the inputs into original, crafted and premeditated outputs.

Such dynamic reflection needs to exist as a habit, which you must encourage and manage. You do this by introducing the trainee to a range of focused experiences, and also by structuring the reflection in your formal and informal meetings. If the trainee isn't making the connections, you need to lead her into doing that. If she isn't evaluating, you need to show her how to do that. And you need to help her crystallise her reflection into action. In other words, you need to support her at all three stages of the process – with a range of inputs, with structured reflection and with focused, consequent future planning.

Watch those targets

We have mentioned targets, and these will be returned to in later chapters. It's worth considering how they might work. A common weakness in training courses is the poor monitoring of targets. Targets are set, and usually these are appropriate, SMART targets (see p. 57) to underpin the trainee's development (see, for example, Chapter 5). This is good and necessary practice; in fact, it's at the heart of a personalised training programme. But very often, that's where the matter rests. Targets are set. A week or a month later, more targets are set. The trainee may, after a few months, be carrying fifty or sixty targets around with her. No one has ever returned to any of these targets, to disapply them as now achieved, or to reinstate them as still pending. In fact, they are quietly forgotten.

A remarkable sense of confidence, purpose and progress can be generated when targets are properly followed up. Here's an example of a simple system for this.

1   *Observation*: During a lesson observation, you note that your trainee needs to expand her repertoire of question types. She tends only to ask closed questions.
2   *Feedback*: You discuss this during feedback. You offer suggestions for a wider range.
3   *Dynamic reflection*: You make some opportunities to explore this topic. These might include observation of other teachers; reading; discussion with other trainees and other staff.
4   *Lesson planning*: The trainee (with your help) decides which classes in the coming week will offer her the chance to use a wider range of question types. When planning these lessons, she indicates at the top of the plan that this target is specifically being addressed.
5   *Observation*: While observing, you have the lesson plan, which reminds you that the questioning target is being addressed. In your observation, you comment on the target (among other things). The cycle begins again – with the same target, if it still needs work, or with a new target.

Who should mentor?

At this point, it might be appropriate to consider whether you want to take on this role. Other chapters later in this book set out guideline character traits, and these are mostly as you would expect them to be. Mentors need to be approachable, flexible, committed. They need to be fascinated by teaching and learning. They need to be experts, but entirely open to new ideas and to reanalysis of their own practices. They need to be prepared and able to be explicit about what they do. They need to be problem-solvers. They need to be realistic but not cynical. They need to be creative and well organised. They need to want to work beyond the level of skilled pragmatism and to see the bigger educational pictures. They need emotional intelligence (see Chapter 5). They need to enjoy collaborative work (see Chapters 3 and 6). This is not a surprising list, but it may well be a challenging one.

If you recognise most (or at least some) of these characteristics in yourself, you should perhaps next consider your proposed mentoring role as it relates to your other duties. Good mentoring is time-consuming. Sometimes, it's also emotionally exhausting. You already have a job that is both of these things. So think carefully.

Senior mentors, also known as *professional* mentors, are often already senior staff members with weighty, whole-school responsibilities. For example, deputy head teachers or senior managers are often required to take on senior mentoring roles as well. It's possible for this to be a mistake. The senior mentor in a secondary school may be the main conduit for training innovation and communications between the external training provider and trainees and other mentors within the school. Overworked managers for whom this is one additional responsibility may not be best placed to fulfil these functions, and the resulting bottlenecks may have serious repercussions.

Similarly, at the subject level within the secondary school, the head of the department or faculty – the 'subject leader' – may not be the best person for the job. He has many other responsibilities and probably a full teaching timetable as well. He may relish the idea of mentoring, and would have much to offer if he had the time to offer it. It's possible for the trainee to feel neglected in such a context, because the mentor has so many distractions and priorities.

Let's consider this difficult issue of priority. The trainee may be working for the first time in a place where she is not the main institutional focus. At school and at university, she was the central priority – the *raison d'être* of the institution. Now she finds herself in an environment where she occupies a position well down the list of essential priorities. The children in your school, for example, are properly much more important than she is.

This is a culture shift for many trainees. Of course, when a student leaves university and gets her first job, she makes a similar change, but it isn't identical. If you work for a bank, the bank is more important than you; it doesn't exist to serve your needs as an employee. But you have some status in that workplace, based on the fact that you are a salaried employee and you chose and were chosen to work there. The trainee is in an oddly ambiguous position in your school, and for many it takes some time to define status and role. In many ways, this is their problem rather than yours, but it may help if you try to remember this ambiguity. The trainee is an adult, but not an employee; she is vulnerable and of low status, but she is not a child. This means that the nature of your relationship with her may be demanding and complex.

Such complexities need time and thought, which is why it might be worth considering that the obvious, more senior individuals may not be best placed for mentoring. Of course, many senior managers make excellent mentors, but some may find it difficult to find the time. If you can't clearly see that you can do this in practical terms, then you shouldn't take it on.

Let's give more positive consideration to other groups within the staff of a school. There are teachers with established talents who may not have sought, or yet achieved, senior managerial posts at departmental or whole-school level. In the UK, they may be known as advanced skills teachers, or excellent teachers, or they may simply be subject teachers with three or four years of successful experience who are seeking to develop their careers. They may be deputy heads of large departments. For such individuals, the development of mentoring within a growing whole-school training profile would be a powerful driver of career progression. It could be attached to gaining higher academic qualifications in partnership with the training provider. Such people are busy, of course: they are teachers. But they may not have a wide portfolio of school responsibilities and may be able to give mentoring the focus it needs and deserves.

Of course, experience and maturity are mentoring assets. Teachers with only a few years of experience may have much to offer, but some occasionally report difficulties. It can be challenging to mentor a mature student who has spent twenty years in insurance if you are only twenty-six yourself. A school with rich mentoring resources (such as whole-mentoring departments – see Chapter 6) will try to allocate appropriate mentors. A particularly young mentor may encounter some resistance, and may need help in establishing working relationships. She needs to gain confidence – after all, she knows more about the job than her trainee does. Clearly established professional routines and expectations are necessary to support new and young mentors. Co-mentoring or coaching (see Chapter 7) may be the way for a new mentor to begin. With time, she will achieve a balance of wisdom and empathy, because she may well have a better and more recent understanding of the trainee's various inevitable predicaments than a more senior colleague.

Later chapters explain co-mentoring and coaching, and it may be worth considering the benefits to both a trainee and a young teacher of setting up mentoring partnerships. A trainee benefits from someone who has time for her and who remembers how training feels, but perhaps she also needs a senior, expert figure. It may be hard for you to be both, but both of those individuals probably exist, and – perhaps as coach and mentor – they can share the mentoring role. There's much more on this in Chapters 6 and 7.

The chapters that follow consider many aspects of mentoring. Chapter 3 considers various versions of collaborative working – the heart of mentoring and very much more than 'team teaching'. In Chapter 4, we look in depth at reflective practice, and Chapter 5 examines aspects of mentoring relationships, with particular reference to the need for emotional intelligence and using transactional-analysis techniques. Chapter 6 considers some interesting versions of group mentoring, including the establishing of whole-mentoring departments. Chapter 7 explains and exemplifies the differences between mentoring and coaching – a creative and fruitful distinction – while in Chapter 8 we look at aspects of mentoring that are specific to primary education. Chapter 9 extends the focus of the book to the mentoring of newly qualified teachers, and, in Chapter 10, trainee teachers offer their frustrations and celebrations with regard to their own experiences of being mentored.

If one theme runs through all of these chapters, it might be that active, reflective and collaborative mentoring isn't only essential to the development of new teachers but is highly beneficial to the professional development and job enjoyment of the mentors themselves.

Chapter 3

Collaborative working

The heart of good mentoring

John Sears

Teaching a class has been an individual exercise for so long that moving into collaborative systems is bound to be something of a culture shift. For some time now, teachers have worked together in departments and faculties and on cross-curricular projects, but the benefits of this spirit of cooperation have taken a while to seep into attitudes towards teacher training. An older model based on 'what happened to me' still pervades the system. For example, it is still common to base training on the belief that 'more is better'. This is founded on the notion that the purpose of the training experience is to recreate incrementally the actual daily life of teaching. Generally, people assume that the more you can do on your own, the better it is. This begs the question of how simply doing more can improve your practice, if you do not know what you are doing to start with? It also assumes that *all* the things a teacher does have to be recreated during the training period – an assumption that we challenged in Chapter 1.

As a result, most training follows a similar kind of pattern. A period of observation is followed by some shared teaching with a mentor (and maybe another trainee). Gradually, the trainee takes over classes until he is left on his own to take full responsibility for his pupils. More and more classes are taken on, and collaborative work, such as observation of other teachers, is systematically reduced. This is often seen as a desirable progression towards independence. But we need to keep returning to the question of how do we *best* learn to do complex tasks?

Trainees are learners

What do we understand about how people learn that we can apply to trainees? When teaching pupils, we would naturally provide a big picture, scaffolding and clear structures into which information could be fitted. We would use a variety of approaches, involving individual and collaborative work, in which children could explore what they needed to learn. We would offer time for reflection. In other words, we would apply notions based on Bruner and Vygotsky and other learning theorists. Yet much of teacher-training practice abandons these ideas and leaves trainees to 'get on with it', whatever the 'it' might be.

The point is that it is the *quality* of the training and not the *quantity* that really matters. This depends, above all else, on the quality of the collaborative relationship between the trainee and the mentor. Success will depend very strongly on the attitude of the mentor to the process. Someone who believes that both she and the trainee have things to learn together is more likely to be able to help a trainee than someone who thinks the process is about monitoring and getting on with it. No one is an expert in every part of the subject she has to teach. Working with another adult allows the mentor, at the very least, an opportunity to learn more about her own subject and to develop her own teaching. I am a biologist, but working as a young head of department with a newly qualified teacher who had vastly more understanding of physiology than I did

was an enormous benefit to me in making the subject come alive to pupils. The new teacher brings a different perspective, not only on the subject, but very often on pupils too. Many trainees have worked previously with children and adults in contexts other than schools. So your trainee can bring ideas on how to approach pupils as well as lesson content. Any mentor who is open to learning from this opportunity is likely to succeed with her trainees. This is at the heart of reflective practice, a term much used but little understood. This reflective relationship has already been highlighted in Chapter 2, and we will return to it again in Chapter 6.

By working collaboratively with trainees to develop their understanding of what a range of successful lessons is like, by selectively structuring their learning experiences and giving them time to understand the frameworks that are available, we can provide a solid basis for good teaching. It is my belief that a first-year teacher who has successfully experienced a variety of lesson types, and has been given the opportunity to reflect upon them through focused discussion and collaboration with a number of colleagues, is able to take on the workload more easily because he understands what he is trying to do. One who comes from the 'more is better' system will often not truly appreciate the possibilities available (because he never had time to!) and will go on producing only routine lessons, just as he did during his training. Inevitably, it will take him longer to develop into a good teacher.

Frameworks

Let's turn now to some of the frameworks available to help us develop our collaborative work. Bruner has long argued for a constructivist approach to learning, and it is helpful to consider his ideas in relation to adults as well as to children. Like a teacher with her class, a mentor needs to provide the optimal experiences to support her trainee. She needs to structure the learning for best comprehension, to provide opportunities for discussion and reflection and to maintain a positive approach to a trainee's successes or (especially) failures.

This positive approach to problems is crucial. Not everything we try works well. Disasters occur, but this is not a reason for not trying again, or for writing off the approach. The mentor and the trainee need to collaborate in the analysis of what went wrong, so that changes can be made which will support the trainee's development.

In this collaborative ethos, classroom failures are not a source of blame or guilt but an essential spur to progress.

Dewey, a precursor of Bruner, also argued that learning was a social process. He argued that all knowledge is about the *relationship* between the knower and the world, and that such relationships mean that the world is neither fully invented, nor fully discovered. He was also at pains to point to the social construction of knowledge for each individual. Through sharing in activities, the trainee gradually acquires a 'mind' of his own. The trainee is not building up knowledge anew on its own account in isolation; he will come to his own final view of the system in which he works if supported by knowledgeable others. The implication of this may seem to be one of rampant subjectivity, but Dewey argues that the social construction of knowledge actively prevents this, because in any transaction each person has to cooperate to try to see the meaning from the viewpoint of other people. This builds a shared meaning of reality and explains a failure of understanding as a failure to come to 'an agreement in action'. This seems to me to be an inherent feature of learning to teach and a basic philosophical position that will help trainees, mentors and tutors to become more successful. Of course, some trainees will find themselves unsuited to the work; but often failure is as much to do with the breakdown of the teaching relationship with the mentor as it is to do with inability – which, incidentally, is often the case with pupil learning!

Vygotsky is another theorist who developed the notion of scaffolding and structured support for learners. Probably his most famous conception is that of the zone of proximal development (ZPD). This is the gap between what a child can do on his own and what he can achieve with support from an adult or *more capable peers* (an idea to return to). This concept is just as valid for an adult learner as for a child. When first working with a trainee, it is important to try to identify what he can already do on his own and then, by working collaboratively, to find out what he can do with help. By practising the latter, the boundaries of the ZPD can be moved forward. In this context, trainees working together (for example, in pairs) can often learn as effectively as those working alongside mentors. Although mentors and tutors worry about the differences between paired individuals, it is unlikely that one will outstrip the other in *all* of the skills required of a teacher, and so either can act as a *more capable peer* for the other. For example, a very organised female trainee who is rather pedestrian in her approach is paired with a very creative male trainee who is chaotic-ally organised. Each learns from the other, and both go on to be very successful teachers. A creative and effective synthesis is achieved. An active mentor will be able to use this paired interaction and she will be able to derive accelerated benefits for both trainees.

So, we have a well-established basis for supposing that learning at all levels has crucial collaborative aspects. We use these ideas with pupils; my argument is that they also apply to trainees.

We have some other frameworks that help us in setting up collaborative events, which have been researched in recent years by a number of training partnerships in the UK. One such approach is based on the thinking of Maslow, whose theories try to take into account many of the affective elements that influence a learner. He developed a hierarchy of the needs that impinge on a learner's motivation (Table 3.1). At its most basic, this hierarchy suggests that, if a learner is cold, hungry and uncomfortable, the chances of her concentrating well on any teaching are severely reduced! At the other end of the scale, a learner will develop 'self actualisation', a state of creative independence focused on solving problems in the real world. Many training courses use this hierarchy in discussing pupils' motivation. Perhaps a consideration of these kinds of influ-ence can help us to understand how to successfully build collab-orative relationships whereby the trainee stays motivated through thick and thin!

At Canterbury Christ Church University College, some work was undertaken to see if this hierarchy could be usefully applied to collaborative work by pairs of trainees placed jointly in a school and subject. The idea was to see if Maslow's framework applied to paired interactions. In general, in what were relatively early days for paired training placements, it seemed that trainees never got much further than the 'security' and 'social' levels of support for one another – what might be called the 'buddy' mode. Trainees were good at reassuring each other and providing a shoulder to cry on, but lacked the confidence to become critical friends. While this is helpful for trainees, it is not enough to justify collaborative systems. This level of relationship can also occur between mentors and trainees, and tutors and trainees, and, although not a bad thing, it is not of itself enough to help trainees develop.

The Canterbury team concluded that, to further enhance progress, conscious and explicit efforts had to be made to teach trainees and mentors how to work collaboratively in a paired placement scheme.

Table 3.1 Maslow's hierarchy of needs

Self-Actualisation
Problem-solving
Realism
Spiritual needs

Autonomy
Independence
Sense of personal freedom

Esteem Needs (ego)
The need for self esteem, achievement,
competence and independence; the need
for recognition and respect from others

Social Needs
The need to love and to be loved, to belong
and be accepted, the need to avoid loneliness and
alienation

Security Needs
The need to feel the world is organised and predictable;
the need to feel safe, secure and stable

Physiological Needs
The need to satisfy hunger and thirst

Some of these possible applications are shown in Table 3.2. The idea was that, eventually, all partners would move to a system where all involved could operate as critical friends (the latter word being of utmost importance!) to ensure mutual development. It is worth considering how to support a new trainee (or a pair of trainees) through the levels of the hierarchy so that they feel reassured, part of the team, esteemed and respected, leading to that higher level of operation that allows self-actualisation. It's also worth considering here that 'partners' in collaborative working may be mentors or other trainees. This is not a mentoring model wholly based on the passing

Table 3.2 Applying Maslow's hierarchy of needs for mentors

Maslow's stage	Type of interaction	Activities
Self-actualisation	'Partner' mode – partners in professional development; critical friends making judgements and suggestions for development; sharing knowledge and understanding	Mutual observation, collaborative teaching, discussion, feedback, joint planning, joint INSET (in-service educational training), joint research and problem-solving
Autonomy	'Appraiser' mode – facilitating the identification of triumphs and tragedies; sharing knowledge and undertaking	Positive critical feedback, allowing experimentation by trainee; trainees to be fully responsible for planning
Esteem	'Counsellor' mode – giving psychological support, e.g. encouragement, warm appreciation, in relation to triumphs and tragedies	Regular and formalised support and meetings; observation with feedback by mentor
Social needs	'Buddy' mode – providing a friendly ear to listen to hopes and fears	
Security Physiological	'Inductor' and 'instructor' modes – sharing basic knowledge, e.g. procedures, locations, etc.	Informal support; meetings and observation by trainee

The table is an adaptation of Field and Philpott's (2001) appropriation of Maslow.

on of expertise from one who knows to one who doesn't, but one that also includes shared experiment and reflection.

Another way to think about collaborative learning is in terms of the types of activity that can be tried as a result of analysing a trainee's needs. Work on this has produced many different ways of grouping things, but one broad framework was devised by Arthur *et al.* (1997), and a modified version is shown in Table 3.3.

Work at the University of Worcester developed the value of these modes of collaboration in relation to the kinds of need that trainees might have. To help structure the approach, we used the stages of development first described by Furlong and Maynard (1995) as

Table 3.3 Modes of collaborative working

Type of collaboration	Explanation	Comment
Observation	One partner watches the other. This can be a focused observation to analyse a particular approach, or may be for the observer to raise questions as feedback.	It could be used for the observer to give feedback, although this is more likely if the pairs are of equal status. With a mentor, this is always used pre-teaching, but there is no reason why it could not be used later for more specific purposes.
Teacher plus learning support assistant (LSA)	In this mode one partner leads and the other acts as LSA. In this model, the LSA can work with an individual, a group with learning difficulties, or the high achievers.	Having a clear lead teacher can allow for modelling a particular approach and can help pupils by ensuring where the centre of authority sits.
Sequential within the lesson	Here the partners compartmentalise the lesson into prearranged sections and take separate responsibility for them. This can help individuals by allowing them to focus on particular skills, e.g. settling the class; conducting a demonstration; summarising, etc.	This can run into problems if people overrun their section and can leave pupils confused as to who is in charge.
Split mode	One partner plans and the other teaches.	This is only effective if the debrief is carried out sensitively but thoroughly.
Class division mode	In this version, the class is split into two, and each partner teaches one half the same content.	This gives more individual attention and allows clear responsibility.

a broad view of the kinds of need that could be found. So, it is quite usual to find that trainees become comfortable with a narrow range of techniques that seem to them to 'work'. Furlong and Maynard call this 'hitting the plateau'. An astute mentor might well ask the trainee at this point to plan a very demanding lesson for her (the mentor) to teach. She will then teach the lesson, while the trainee observes. Joint discussion can then lead to the trainee attempting something of this sort with another group.

For example, many science trainees become comfortable with contextualising a topic, setting up an experiment and concluding from it whatever it is they want pupils to learn. This is a perfectly good strategy for some topics, or parts of topics. However, if repeated every lesson, it risks becoming dull and incoherent for pupils. A mentor might therefore ask the trainee to plan a lesson involving a circus of experiments, or a simulation, which she can then teach to show her expanded repertoire. In these ways, the trainee can move beyond the plateau.

Furlong and Maynard also helpfully categorised other states of development of trainees that can be used to analyse trainees' needs. For example, trainees may appear to be in 'survival mode', where their attention is solely given to behavioural issues, rather than seeing the bigger picture that links planning and appropriateness to behaviour. They may be focused on particular difficulties they are having, or particular pupils, at the expense of other important issues. This kind of awareness is needed by the mentor so that she can bring this into discussion with the trainee and create appropriate challenges so that he can move forward.

So, we can see that there are a variety of frameworks that can help us to develop collaborative work. Most learning theories and theories of motivation are grounded in the need for collaboration and in the fact that we are a social species. We apply this commonly in the ways in which we approach teaching pupils, and the same systems work equally well for adult learners. We are talking here of a range of activities, in which the collaboration may usefully be between trainee and mentor or between trainee and trainee. In Table 3.4, we can see a spread of activities covering lesson planning and teaching. In any of these, collaborator A or B may be trainee or mentor.

One final thought on frameworks, before moving on to some examples of applying the ideas, concerns the language of training. Language is what creates our shared meanings in life. It is how we

Table 3.4 Collaborative working

Theme	Focus	A	B
Lesson planning	Parts of a lesson based on agreed learning objectives	Plans the starter and plenary	Plans the main activities
	Using learning objectives	Decides on appropriate objectives	Plans the lesson
	Group work	Decides on appropriate objectives	Devises appropriate group work
	Questioning in lesson with agreed outline	Devises main activities	Focuses on a range of appropriate questioning
	Health and safety on agreed lesson outline	Highlights health and safety issues in plan	Focuses on solutions to these issues
	Differentiation in lesson with agreed learning objectives	Devises outline plan	Modifies plan for enhanced differentiation
	Inclusion in lesson with agreed learning objectives	Devises outline plan	Modifies plan for enhanced inclusion
	Focusing on pupils' reactions and experiences	Devises outline plan	Considers effectiveness of use of pupils' attitudes and experiences
	Understanding transitions in lesson with agreed outline	Devises key activities	Focuses on key transitions between activities
	Working on English as an additional language (EAL) on agreed lesson outline	Devises key activities	Modifies plan for enhanced EAL
	Evaluation of lesson with agreed outline	Devises starter and main activities	Focuses on evaluation throughout and on plenary activity

Table 3.4 (continued)

Theme	Focus	A	B
Planning and teaching	Lesson planning	Plans lesson	Teaches lesson
	Feedback	Teaches	Observes and gives feedback
	Teaching a jointly planned lesson	Teaches starter, plenary	Teaches main activities
		Acts as teacher	Acts as teaching assistant, e.g. for SEN or EAL
		Teaches half the class	Teaches half the class
		Teaches most of class	Teaches specific small group
		Teaches and supervises whole class	Takes smaller groups for guided group work
	Teaching a sequence of lessons	Plans and teaches lesson 1	Plans and teaches lesson 2
		Plans lesson 1, teaches lesson 2	Teaches lesson 1, plans lesson 2
Medium- and short-term planning	Creating a short-term plan	Draws the plan objectives from the medium-term plan and creates short-term overview	Plans individual lessons to objectives; gathers resources
	Resources	Creates overview of short- or medium-term plan	Lists necessary resources for plan and allocates resource creation tasks to A and B
	Creating a medium-term plan	Draws learning objectives from long-term plan; discusses with B; divides short-term planning between A and B	Creates half of the short-term plans, as allocated, and evaluates scheme before and after teaching

Table 3.4 (contnued)

Theme	Focus	A	B
Behaviour management	Planning for good behaviour	Plans a lesson to agreed objectives	Evaluates lesson plan; looks for danger zones; looks for motivation and interest points; checks level and appropriateness; modifies plan for good behaviour
	Teaching	Teaches	Observes with behaviour focus
	Discussion of approaches in teaching	Tries a very formal approach	Tries (and compares) an informal approach
	Beginnings	Plans and teaches	Observes and evaluates beginnings – of lesson and of each section
	On-task behaviour	Teaches	Observes and records on- and off-task behaviour
Assessment	Marking work	Sets marking criteria; marks jointly; marks batch of work; writes comments; writes positive comments; writes developmental comments	Marks to criteria; marks jointly; second-marks sample; grades to criteria; writes developmental comments; writes engaged comments
	Assessment for learning	Marks work; sets work	Develops next lesson; discusses work with pupil; sets up peer assessment criteria
		Takes an overview of single pupil's work	Sets a level or grade for single pupil's work

conceptualise the world and come to see what others see. In the context of any learning, use of language therefore has especial significance. It is helpful that trainees, mentors and tutors have a common understanding of the terminology that they are using and of what this means for their view of the educational world. Of course, in a field as diverse as education, complete agreement is probably impossible, but certain fundamentals need to be agreed. In writing this book, we have chosen to use the word *trainee* because we believe this has the widest currency at present. However, it could lead readers to suppose that we believe learning to teach is just about *training,* rather than *education.* This, of course, is not our intent, but it gives some indication of the complexities and pitfalls of educational language. *Top set* implies *bottom set*; *special needs child* is an insulting label rather than an analysis; how we talk about what we do informs, reveals and affects our attitudes. Partnerships need to work together to have a shared philosophy and a core language, as this helps trainees to understand and develop their own worldpicture of education and schooling.

Some examples

My argument is that quality of experience is more important than quantity; that collaboration is fundamental; that ideas we apply to pupils' learning apply equally well to trainees, and that various frameworks can be used to help us give trainees success as beginning teachers. So now let us look at some specific examples of collaborative work, bearing in mind that we are considering collaboration both between trainee and trainee, and between trainee and mentor.

One science trainee was given three Year 8 classes to teach during his first school placement. This was a little problematic since, even though the groups were differentiated by attainment and achievement, they were being taught the same topic. However, the mentor made good use of the opportunity by having the trainee observe a lesson being taught by himself. The trainee was then asked to teach the same lesson to the next group using the mentor's lesson plan. The trainee then devised his own version of the lesson for the third group. In fact, this opportunity was very instructive for the trainee and gave him real experience on which to base decisions about his own teaching style and to engage in a debate with the mentor about the appropriateness of different approaches for pupils of different achievement levels. The trainee ended up teaching a very different lesson from his mentor, who was fairly traditional in his approach, but one that both recognised as being successful in terms of pupil learning.

This small example shows how the frameworks of collaboration can be incorporated into a straightforward but powerful sequence of learning experiences for the trainee. It also shows how collaboration can operate at a high level within Maslow's hierarchy. Collaboration in this case wasn't 'team teaching'; it was collaborative *planning*.

Another example of successful collaboration comes from a pair of geography trainees, one of whom was clearly more confident than the other. Many people express doubts about a pairing that is unbalanced in this way, fearing that the stronger trainee will be held back, or will do the work *for* the other, whose inabilities will only later come to the fore. But this does not have to happen, and the sequences below show that effective mentor choices, exploiting the opportunities that presented themselves, extended the strengths and remediated the weaknesses of both trainees. These choices are not complex, but they require a little thought.

The mentor in this case was committed to applying the frameworks we have discussed. The initial work consisted of a mapping exercise conducted in the school grounds. The work was planned for two classes, and the higher-achieving group came earlier in the week.

What mattered was the progressive sequencing of the work. The work was *planned fully by the teacher* and explained in detail to the trainees. The teacher led the lesson introduction up to the point where the pupils went outside. For the higher-achieving class, pupils were then divided into three groups. The best-motivated pupils were put into two small groups, each led by one of the trainees. The less-motivated half of the class was taken out by the mentor.

Later in the week, with the more challenging group, the mentor divided the class into two. She selected the better-behaved pupils to work with her teaching assistant (TA) and the more confident trainee, and she herself took the more difficult pupils with the less confident trainee. This enabled the trainees to gain experience of different approaches needed for the same work, with pupils of differing attitudes and achievement levels.

The mentor followed this with a further class division exercise where all three worked in the same large room. This class was an unstreamed group of 11–12-year-olds. The mentor led the lesson, which featured a model-making exercise for pupils in which they were to produce globes. The trainees each supervised one quarter of the group where the pupils made their model globes, while the other half of the class was being taught by the mentor. Halfway through, the arrangement was swapped over. The mentor had planned the lesson overview, but she let the trainees plan how to manage the modelling section. They had close supervision of a practical activity (scissors, glue and all those tempting things for young children!), but with a small group, so that they could safely learn about activities that can be difficult to manage.

The mentor commented:

> I think they learned a lot about mixed ability and different abilities in children and they learned a bit more about management and a bit of lesson planning . . . they had to start thinking about what they were doing, why they were doing it, what they were trying to get the children to learn from it and what they wanted to talk to them about within the context of the scheme of work.

The pupils were also taken out to visit a sandstone church to look at weathering. The mentor planned the work but required the trainees to act as TAs when out at the site. This proved to be a valuable learning experience in relation both to planning visits and to how to interact with pupils in less formal settings.

The mentor commented:

> I felt that that was a really useful opportunity for them to get in there and talk to children in a totally different context and see the problems of over-familiarity which tend to creep in when you are outside.

The next step was for each trainee to do a starter and a plenary session. The starters and plenaries were jointly planned by the trainees after discussion with the mentor about the overall lesson content and objectives. The mentor commented:

> They each just did a plenary and just a starter, so if it was a disaster it was a ten-minute disaster and they didn't have to worry about that.

The mentor next asked the trainees to plan a lesson for her to teach. This proved very interesting, as they put in far too much for the time available. The mentor tried to stick to the plan, but only taught part of what was there, having to invent a different homework! The trainees observed the lesson and fed back on what they had seen. They were then asked jointly to plan the next lesson for the group, which they would teach in sequential mode. This time they planned a more appropriate length of lesson. However, when they came to teach it, they finished it in about twenty minutes. The mentor then needed to step in and take over the lesson to help reinforce the work and establish that pupils had actually understood what they were doing.

These two trainees had different mixtures of modules in their degrees. One was a human geographer, and the other a physical geographer. The mentor utilised this by requiring each to plan within her area of relative weakness and to be observed by the other. In this way, each tutored the other, to help the development of subject knowledge.

These complex and progressive models are a far cry from simple, traditional versions of collaborative working, which are often limited to 'team-teaching' and observation-plus-feedback. This training sequence led to discussions of key issues, such as the depth of material, the need for reinforcement, assessment for learning and appropriate activities. These experiences happened early in the trainees' year, but the level of their discussion was heightened by the mentor's careful structuring of experiences and the degree of collaboration between three qualified adults.

What we see here is the careful application of the ideas of collaboration. The mentor concluded that it was time-consuming but worth it. She spent more time with the trainees than one would normally do early on, but this gave the trainees more confidence and independence in the long term, thus eventually saving time and ensuring that the quality of their input was better, sooner. When they returned for a training period at the university, their tutor found them to be well ahead of their peers in their levels of understanding. At the end of the year, both trainees said they had benefited from those early experiences and had been able to use collaborative approaches in their final school placement to help their learning, both with mentors and other trainees – even from other subjects. The weaker of the two trainees is clear that, without that successful first experience, she may well not have gone on to qualify.

So far, the examples of collaboration have come from early on in the training year. Many people think this is fine, but that, as the year progresses, far more individual work should be done. Consequently, it is common for collaboration to diminish through the training period. At the University of Worcester, we have developed a different pattern of training on our flexible Post-graduate Certificate in Education (PGCE) course. On flexible courses, most trainees have fewer taught sessions and work on structured tasks in schools instead. This is a kind of distance learning, and, with a reduced amount of tutor-led central training, they derive support by working in pairs and in larger groups. Of course, they teach individually, but they also continue throughout the training to teach collaboratively and to work on tasks and assignments collaboratively. The culture of collaboration engendered from this arrangement is significantly different from the experiences of trainees on other courses, and the hope is that this will be carried through into their early teaching posts.

Conclusions

The examples above are, of course, small-scale ones. However, there is now an increasing body of evidence from across the world about paired placements and collaborations with mentors that shows overwhelmingly the benefits for trainees, and consequently for pupils. There is also evidence about collaborative group mentoring (see Chapter 6). Learning appears to be quicker and of better quality when people work together. This really should not come as a surprise! Learning is also improved when experiences are structured and tailored to individual need; we know this as teachers, but have been slow to apply the idea to learning to be a teacher. Moreover, the evidence puts paid once and for all to the myth that teachers are 'born and not made'. Of course, we recognise that some qualities needed to be a good teacher may occur naturally in some trainees and not in others; but they can be developed. In the case of our geographers, one trainee would almost certainly have left the course without that first, very supportive, carefully contrived, collaborative experience. She has gone on to become a good teacher and was able, even while training, to bring collaborative ideas into her own practice, which helped support mentors and other trainees.

Dealing with failure

One of the main features of good collaborative work that has become apparent to me, in thirty-five years of work in education, is that it is how you deal with failure that really makes the difference. This is true as much with pupils and trainees as it is with experienced teachers. I can still remember being told by one of my first science groups that they were too stupid to do the work I'd set, because I'd set this same experiment to the top set, and they were *remedials* (the school's own categorisation in those days). Failure was their expectation, because it was what their teachers thought. It is surprisingly easy for adults to get into the same mindset if they are castigated and labelled by their tutors or mentors. Yet, all trainees will have failures. Even experienced teachers still have bad days. When one of our lessons goes wrong, we do not (normally) feel that the end of the world has come, or that the pupils' educational experience has been irretrievably ruined. Trainees, with their lack of experience and (thus) of perspective, are likely to be disproportionate in their reactions to problems. We need to remember this when we are working with them and to stay proportionate on their behalf. It is clear that, by working more closely and collaboratively, we can reduce the risk of bad lessons and analyse failure supportively, so that trainees do not lose confidence.

By recognising that there are frameworks in which to think about our work, and ways of applying this, all mentors, continuing professional development (CPD) coordinators and tutors can raise the quality of training. I cannot prove, at this time, that quality is absolutely more important than quantity, but it seems to me that the onus is on those who believe in an older, non-collaborative model to demonstrate its effectiveness compared with a more reflective experience. One thing we know for all learners is that they need time to integrate new experiences and frameworks and language to help them. If all they have time to do is churn out another bog-standard lesson, they will not have time to make sense of what they are doing. They will fail to value the joys of teaching and learning, and so, inevitably, will their pupils.

References

Arthur, J., Davison, J. and Moss, J. (1997) *Subject mentoring in the secondary school,* London and New York: Routledge.

Field, K. and Philpott, C. (2001) 'Mentoring in schools: from support to development', in A. Edwards, *Supporting personal advisers in Connexions: perspectives on supervision and mentoring from allied professions,* Canterbury: Canterbury Christ Church University.

Furlong, J. and Maynard, T. (1995) *Mentoring student teachers,* London: Routledge.

Chapter 4

Reflective practice

The mentoring conversation

Alison Winson and Sue Wood-Griffiths

> A learning conversation is a planned and systematic approach to professional dialogue that supports teachers to reflect on their practice. As a result the teacher gains new knowledge and uses it to improve his or her teaching.
>
> General Teaching Council for England (2004)

Teaching is an exciting profession, and being a mentor can add a further dimension to your work, with the challenges, frustrations and discoveries that arise from supporting a trainee teacher's development. You will observe lessons where you think, 'What a brilliant idea!', and others where your reaction will be, 'How on earth can I help her to get this right?'. The learning conversations that take place between the trainee and the mentor are vital to supporting the new teacher, developing her confidence and encouraging her to determine how to move on. The feedback you give, the language you choose and the questions that you pose are critical, and the nature of these conversations, as well as their content, is crucial to successful mentoring.

Trainee teachers aren't children, but, in many ways, the relationship between the mentor and the trainee productively parallels that between teacher and pupil. For example, in recent years in the UK, there has been a focus in schools on Assessment for Learning (AfL), where pupils have been encouraged to reflect on their work and, helped by their teachers, to identify where and how they can improve. The process of mentoring a trainee teacher could be seen to adopt the same strategy, and direct parallels can be drawn between the assessment of pupils and the feedback given to trainee teachers. The focus of this chapter will be on the crucial part played by the conversations between the mentor and the trainee in developing her teaching and wider professional role.

Developing independence

The complex relationship between a mentor and trainee starts from the point of initial contact. First impressions will influence the future professional relationship of both parties, and it is important to both that these are positive. Positive feedback from a mentor on first meeting a trainee ('I was interested to read that you went to school in Harrogate . . .') can quickly put her at ease and help form the basis of a trusting relationship that will enable honest praise and criticism in the future. Developing confidence is a precursor to developing independence.

Trainee teachers are generally anxious at the start of their practice and focus largely on themselves and their performance. They tend to look to the mentor imploringly with questions such as, 'How was it? How have I done?'. They are seeking reassurance, though they are often largely unaware of the skills they need to develop. Early on in the development of a trainee teacher, therefore, feedback is likely to be focused on developing confidence, with much encouragement and praise, balanced with constructive advice about the fundamentals of lesson planning and delivery.

The process of *feeding back* to a trainee teacher is a crucial one at this early stage (and throughout the training). However, the term *feedback* is interpreted by people in very different ways. Some see it as a one-way process where the mentor talks and the trainee listens. In this instance, feedback becomes a relatively passive process for the trainee.

Some mentors start the dialogue by asking initial questions such as, 'How do you think the lesson went?' or 'If you taught the lesson again, what would you do differently?'. This at least allows the trainee the opportunity to begin the process of reflection, and starting with such questions is a good discipline for the mentor. All too often, however, this is the end of the two-way conversation, and the trainee becomes passive again as the mentor proceeds to read his comments straight from the observation sheet.

We see the most productive type of feedback as a conversation that develops between the two participants. *If mentors are going to develop a trainee teacher's reflective practice, then the evaluative responsibility must be passed to her.* The most straightforward response, as we've said, is to ask whether the lesson was successful, and in what ways it could be improved. Properly sustained, this approach compels the trainee teacher to think for herself about her strengths and weaknesses and starts a dialogue where the mentor might affirm or challenge her ideas. As trainees move on through the training, the questions can become more challenging in scope and serve to shift trainees' thinking away from themselves as teachers, towards their pupils and their pupils' learning.

Trainees and learning theory

Most trainees are going to encounter learning theories. If we can encourage them to apply these theories to their *own* learning as well as to that of their pupils, we can start to develop their reflective practice. We mentioned these parallels in Chapter 3.

When students look at the *constructivist* theories of learning, they readily relate to Vygotsky's (1986) theories. One of these ideas, which is particularly pertinent, is his concept of a zone of proximal development (ZPD), which describes the gap between what a learner can do alone and what he can achieve with support. We discussed aspects of this theory in Chapter 3. Vygotsky also places great emphasis on language, and particularly talk, as central to the development of thinking. Obviously, the ZPD places the teacher in a crucial place for developing her pupils. The mentor may helpfully be seen to be in a similar relationship with her trainee. But, to better consider the relevance of the ZPD to the work of the mentor, we need to consider and interrogate some more models of learning.

The *conscious competence* model, sometimes credited to W. S. Howell (1982), describes a four-stage model of learning (see Table 4.1). This is sometimes represented as a ladder.

Table 4.1 The conscious competence model

Stage 4	Unconscious competence
Stage 3	Conscious competence
Stage 2	Conscious incompetence
Stage 1	Unconscious incompetence

At the bottom is stage 1, described as *unconscious incompetence*. At stage 1:

- the trainee teacher is not aware of the existence or relevance of the skill area she needs to develop;
- the trainee teacher is not aware that she has a particular deficiency in the area;
- the trainee teacher might deny the relevance of the new skill;
- the trainee teacher must become conscious of her incompetence before development of the skill can begin;
- the aim of the trainee teacher and the mentor is to move on to the 'conscious competence' stage, by demonstrating the benefit that it will bring to the trainee teacher's effectiveness.

At stage 2, described as *conscious incompetence*, the trainee's thinking has moved on, and now:

- the trainee teacher becomes aware of the existence and relevance of the skill;
- the trainee teacher is therefore also aware of her deficiency in this area, perhaps through trying unsuccessfully to use the skill;
- the trainee teacher realises that, by improving her skill in this area, she will increase her effectiveness;

- the trainee teacher has a measure of the extent of her deficiency in the relevant skill, and a measure of what level of skill is required for her own competence;
- the trainee teacher makes a commitment to learn and practise the new skill, and to move to the 'conscious competence' stage.

At Stage 3, which is described as *conscious competence*, we begin to see an improvement in the trainee teacher's practice. Here:

- the trainee teacher achieves 'conscious competence' in a skill when she can perform it at will;
- the trainee teacher will need to concentrate and think in order to perform the skill;
- the trainee teacher can perform the skill without assistance;
- the trainee teacher will not reliably perform the skill unless thinking about it – the skill is not yet 'second nature' or 'automatic';
- the trainee teacher should continue to practise the new skill, and commit to becoming 'unconsciously competent' at the new skill.

Practice is the single most effective way to move from stage 3 to stage 4, the final stage, which is described as *unconscious competence*, or mastery. Here:

- the skill becomes so practised that it enters the unconscious parts of the brain – it becomes 'second nature';
- it becomes possible for certain skills to be performed while doing something else;
- the trainee might now be able to teach others the skill concerned, although, after some time of being unconsciously competent, she might actually have difficulty in explaining exactly how she does it – the skill has become largely instinctive.

In Chapter 1, we suggested an analogy between learning to teach and learning to drive. At first, the processes of manipulating the gear lever, clutch and steering wheel at the same time are sufficient challenges for a learner, without thinking about mirrors, windscreen wipers, lights and indicators! However, as you continue to learn and practise driving, these things become automatic, and an experienced driver does them without thinking – until presented with challenging driving conditions (or another car), when he may temporarily become more conscious about what he is doing.

If we see the mentor as largely operating at stages 3 and 4 of the model, we can see how he may be able to draw a trainee up through the lower stages by establishing a dialogue and by asking the right questions to move her on through the ZPD. One additional benefit of this for the mentor is that, as he starts negotiating strategies and targets for his trainee, he starts to reflect on his own competence and to identify explicitly what it is that he does that makes him successful. This process, then, can be motivating and rewarding for the mentor as he acknowledges his own skills.

This model can be applied to any aspect of a trainee teacher's work to develop her repertoire of skills – for example, in the use of learning objectives, the development of behaviour management or the skilful design of lesson transitions.

Motivation

Of course, such developments can't happen without motivation. Trainees (and mentors) will naturally be considering theories about motivation and self-esteem in relation to children. Once again, significant progress can be made by applying these theories to the development of the trainee teacher, as well as that of the pupils.

A trainee teacher became embarrassed when a challenging student had accidentally called her 'Mum'. After a difficult start with this class, the trainee had worked hard to establish the right climate in her lessons. She had created a very positive environment by noticing good work and behaviour and rewarding them. It was evident that the class was enjoying her lessons, but this individual pupil's response had completely bewildered her.

When discussing this, the mentor said that it probably showed that the pupil felt 'at home' in the lesson. This gave the trainee teacher a huge sense of achievement, as she realised that she had got to where she aspired to be with the class. In so advising and reassuring her, the mentor had helped her to become *consciously competent*, and this conversation expanded the trainee's confidence and motivation as well as her understanding.

Initially, this trainee was unaware that the pupils in the class as a whole were resistant to her (they had long-established relationships and liked their usual teacher). As she took over the class and attempted to clarify her expectations, they demonstrated this resistance by not cooperating. To support the trainee in improving the situation, the mentor had to help her to realise that it was not her teaching that was the problem, but the fact that the class was unsettled. Once her understanding had been raised in this way, the trainee was able to see that she needed to persist with her expectations and notice and acknowledge the pupils who were cooperating, until the majority had adapted to her and were again settled. Only when the relationships were established would she be able to really achieve what she wanted to with them. In fact, it could be argued that the actions taken by the trainee moved the *pupils* up the conscious-competence ladder, as they became more aware of their learning behaviour, until they were unconsciously operating to meet her expectations. Her growing understanding of the difficulties that she faced and of her pupils' behaviour led directly to a growth in confidence and motivation.

What should be recorded during a lesson observation?

An observation sheet serves many purposes. For all the stakeholders involved in the training, lesson observation is a method of monitoring. Lesson observation sheets reassure the training provider that lessons are being systematically observed. They also serve as a check on the quality of training being offered by a school. They are useful for recording targets, which can be appraised later, and they are (of course) assessment tools for the mentor to record the performance of the trainee, as well as useful records for the trainee in monitoring his own progress.

It is always good to highlight what has gone well – for example, to annotate comments with ticks or smiley faces as recognition of positive aspects of a lesson. Even if the lesson is disappointing, there should always be something that we can highlight as being positive. Unfortunately, however, we do read observation sheets that contain only negative comments. This often happens for the best of motives, but trainee teachers understandably find it demoralising.

On the other hand, we read balanced observation sheets that feature many positive statements as well as identifying areas to improve. Unfortunately, it's not uncommon for the trainee, in reading such an even-handed critique, to see only criticism. The praise is not recognised, or it is ignored. When this happens, it is useful to suggest that the trainee should reread the observation sheet carefully and highlight all of the positive statements.

In fact, the lesson observation sheet is an intricate and complex document. It must focus on the planning of the lesson, the preparation of the room and resources, and the accuracy and level of subject knowledge that have been demonstrated, as well as on the delivery. The sheet will draw attention to achievements and deficiencies with regard to criteria such as (in the UK) the Standards for Qualified Teacher Status. It will comment on the strength of the lesson plan, with regard to clear learning objectives, task-setting and evaluation and assessment strategies. It will refer to the pupils' behaviour, preferably in connection with the planning and learning decisions taken by the trainee. It will evaluate pedagogy and professionalism. It may comment on agreed targets that have already been set.

Such a complex and challenging document cannot simply be handed to the trainee. She cannot expect to make sense of such a range of comment without a careful, accompanying conversation. For example, sometimes a mentor might offer alternative ideas on the observation form, and this may be seen by the trainee teacher as untimely criticism. We have sometimes heard trainees comment, 'Why didn't she offer me that idea beforehand, when she read my lesson plan?'. Trainee teachers need to understand that better solutions sometimes only arise when you see a lesson, rather than when reviewing the plans. Such understanding depends upon the feedback dialogue that surrounds the feedback sheet.

When is the best time to give feedback?

Some mentors feed back to trainee teachers immediately after a lesson, some on the same day, and some later than that. We have spent time discussing with trainee teachers what they consider is the best time to receive feedback. Their immediate response is that they prefer feedback immediately after the lesson. However, as they reflect on the question, they acknowledge that having some delay between the lesson and the feedback provides time for their own reflections, particularly if the lesson has provoked an emotional response in them, such as elation or despair. In these situations, asking the trainee teacher to write her own evaluation of the lesson before feedback can be advantageous and can create a richer mentoring conversation.

More often than not, verbal feedback happens when both the trainee and the mentor have some free time together. It is frustrating for trainees to have to wait days for this – especially for those with a *Hurry Up!* driver (see Chapter 5). This can happen because a mentor is busy, or because she insists on writing her feedback up 'in neat'. This really isn't necessary – no one is checking your handwriting. We have made a plea to mentors not to type or rewrite their feedback. This can often remove the spontaneity of the initial response. Trainee teachers do comment that, if the gap between the lesson and feedback is longer than a day, then they may forget aspects of the lesson itself, and so the developmental value is reduced. Quick feedback means that they can quickly act on suggestions in order to aid their progress.

Asking helpful questions

The asking and answering of questions demand serious thinking from trainee teachers. Throughout their training, and particularly early in the process, they are likely to need support in developing questions about their own and observed practice. In the early stages, the mentor will fulfil a role in training the trainee to assess himself.

Appropriate questioning is what is most likely to move trainees on through their zone of proximal development. In the same way that pupils need to be taught how to employ AfL strategies, trainee teachers need to be trained how to interrogate practice. One way of supporting them to ask developmental questions is by using their observations of other teachers. All trainee teachers are encouraged to observe skilled and experienced colleagues. If they can be encouraged to ask questions about what they observe, a dialogue about teaching and learning can take place. This discussion can not only develop the trainee teacher's understanding of how a lesson might be organised, or of how a particular group of pupils might be managed, but it may also engage the teacher who has been observed in explicitly reflecting on his own practice and acknowledging his own unconscious competence. As this process develops, continuous appraisal of what the trainee teacher is doing and observing becomes routine.

Questions that a mentor can focus on during feedback should emerge from the lesson observation. It is useful to record these questions on the observation form. You might suggest that these questions be used by the trainee to frame an evaluation of the lesson.

Below are some general questions you might want to ask the trainee during feedback.

- What went well in the lesson? How do you know?
- What would enable you to progress further in your teaching?
- What targets would you set yourself, having planned, taught and assessed the lesson?
- How did you personalise the learning of individuals? Were the strategies used successful?
- What did the pupils learn? How do you know?
- How was the learning assessed? How effective was the assessment strategy? How do you know?
- How effective were the resources you used? How do you know they were or were not effective?
- How was pace achieved in the lesson?
- How did you manage the transitions between tasks? Could this have been more effective?
- In which part of the lesson did you feel most confident? Explain why.
- What strategies did you use to manage behaviour? Were these methods effective? What would you do differently next lesson?
- Are there any other ways in which the learning could be assessed?
- How would you rate your explanations? Why?

Setting targets

If a mentoring conversation is to develop a trainee teacher's practice, it is important that targets are set. Training is not the linear acquisition of predetermined skills. It is essentially individual: new teachers move at different speeds and even in different directions. Target-setting is at the heart of this personalised development. At the end of each feedback, a summary of the targets that have emerged during the conversation will help clarify areas for further development for both the trainee teacher and the mentor. Targets should be discussed and recorded. They should be negotiated and refined from the feedback conversation.

Writing clear targets is a skill in itself. We often read observation sheets that have been completed in great detail by mentors but do not include targets. There may be several reasons for this. First, if the trainee teacher is highly skilled, it might be difficult for the mentor to identify a target for improvement. Second, because targets are sometimes difficult to clarify, they are evaded. However, they are essential tools in supporting a trainee teacher to make progress.

As with pupils, the targets the trainee teacher and the mentor negotiate should be SMART. This means that they should be

- Specific
- Measurable
- Attainable
- Realistic
- Time indicated.

All targets should include some strategies to support the trainee teacher in being successful. It is not appropriate to write vague, abstract targets, such as 'You need to increase the pace of your teaching'. Such a target is difficult for the trainee teacher to unravel. It is unlikely that she will understand or will have developed enough skill in the craft of teaching to know how to achieve this – indeed, if she had, it probably wouldn't be an appropriate target anyway. Strategies indicating *how* to increase the pace of a lesson need to be given. These might include giving clear time guidelines for the completion of activities; giving frequent time reminders; organising resources before the start of the lesson and trying to have pupils working as soon as possible. The target may actually relate to the number and variety of activities within the lesson and to the nature of tasks and task-setting. In other words, what looks like a simple target arising from a straightforward observation may well be a complex and subtle matter that needs analysis by the mentor as well as the trainee.

Identifying targets can often prove difficult even for experienced teachers, because they operate with unconscious competence. An experienced teacher will have an instinctive understanding of pace, but nevertheless may find it difficult to articulate this to a trainee. Analysing how to achieve a target such as this is challenging but good professional development for a mentor.

Other common targets that need clarification by a mentor might include how to:

- use the voice more effectively;
- give clearer explanations;
- use praise more constructively;
- ensure full and successful transitions between activities;
- show more enthusiasm;
- challenge pupils;
- be more assertive.

Explanations of how to achieve a target should include exemplification or even a performance from the mentor. Often, demonstrating ('modelling') how to achieve a target can be much more effective than writing strategies. We often demonstrate how to show enthusiasm or how to use the voice more effectively using the analogy of a sports commentary. We can all recognise growing excitement from a football or horse-racing commentator, and using this familiar example with a trainee teacher can help her to make her voice more interesting and varied and to generate some enthusiasm and excitement in her lessons. Such approaches are learned, not from written feedback, but from the mentoring conversation. Table 4.2 exemplifies how key training targets may be broken down into their component parts to make them accessible to a trainee.

It's not uncommon for targets to be lost. They are set and exemplified, but not monitored. Over the training period, they accumulate and disappear; nobody checks whether they have been met. The list grows, nothing is ever crossed off, and the trainee unsurprisingly begins to ignore it. This represents a major weakness in the training, the loss of a crucial opportunity for individual development. *Targets should always be followed up* in the next few lessons or during a review meeting. Systematic tracking of a small number of targets through a week or two of lesson-planning and mentor-observation is surprisingly rare but extraordinarily effective. Progress can be measured and monitored, with even small improvements being acknowledged to motivate the trainee teacher. This process is exemplified in Chapter 2.

How many targets are too many?

Overloading a trainee teacher with too many targets will overwhelm her; it is likely that she will not know which ones to address first. Mentors must filter and prioritise targets that have been set for a trainee teacher. If she is going to be able to demonstrate that she has made progress, limiting targets to a manageable two or three is probably best practice. If a significant number of targets are emerging from a trainee teacher's lessons, you will have to decide what should be a priority. For example, if low-level disruption within a class is not being managed during a lesson, should you be focusing the trainee on a higher-order target centred on differentiation?

Focusing and commenting on these targets in subsequent lessons is helpful to the trainee teacher. The original target can then be developed or acknowledged as having been met.

Remembering to praise trainees for achieving targets successfully is important to ensure they have a sense of achievement and feel they are making progress. If a target is proving difficult to address, then breaking it down into smaller sub-targets might be a useful strategy to render it more realistic. For example, if a trainee teacher is following a standards or competencies model of training, setting a particular *standard* as a target might be inappropriate, whereas breaking it down into smaller components and targeting it in stages might better support her. Where a standards model of training is in place, standards can become a hindrance. The trainee's own specific needs must come first.

What happens if a trainee cannot meet a target or is not listening to advice?

Sometimes, despite your best efforts, you seem to be setting the same target lesson after lesson. Apparently, the trainee does not listen to, or act upon, the advice given to her. There are several reasons why this might happen.

Table 4.2 Setting specific targets

Area to work on	Suggestions
Use of voice	Ensure that you vary the volume and the pitch of your voice, along with the speed of delivery (think of sports commentaries). Avoid shouting, which can lead to your voice sounding shrill. Aim to breathe from your diaphragm and project your voice. Imagine yourself yawning in order to get a deeper sound. Make sure that your voice does not come across as sarcastic or sound patronising to pupils.
Increase pace	Timed activities. Focus on learning rather than teaching. Clear, 'snappy' content. Use starters and plenaries. Share learning objectives and refer to them during the lesson. Monitor that pupils are on task. Organise resources. Give shorter rather than longer deadlines. Be clear as to what you want pupils to have completed by the end of a lesson. Plan a variety of activities. Get pupils on task as quickly as possible. Give frequent time checks to pupils. Break down tasks into manageable units. Go for smooth transitions between tasks. Know pupils' names and direct questions to them.
Give clear instructions	Keep these short but concise. Repeat them several times in different ways. Put the key things pupils need to do on the board to reinforce. Ensure pupils know how to structure their work. Use questioning to check understanding. Pick up/be aware of misconceptions and remedy. Use modelling. Judge number of instructions – not too many at once. Ask pupils to repeat instructions to check they have understood. Use appropriate vocabulary. Visual instructions.
Give praise	Give lots of praise, but make sure that it sounds sincere. Using praise before a reprimand can be very effective (e.g. I know that you can be sensible, but I don't like the way you are . . .). If pupils cannot get attention for doing positive things, they will seek attention for doing negative things, and it is quicker to get the latter!
Set time limits	Give written as well as verbal timings. Start and end your lesson promptly. It is good role modelling. Always give a time limit for a task. Give the pupils less time than you think they need. Count down the time (with urgency). Give them a warning towards the end to focus them on finishing. Avoid dead time. When off task, pupils will start to misbehave. Try using egg-timer, stop-clock, music, etc.

Table 4.2 continued

Area to work on	Suggestions
	Practise how long things take. Put time targets on the board.
Ensure smooth transitions	Give out the next task before pupils have finished or while they are working. Use your learning objectives as a map for the lesson to avoid pauses while you look at your lesson plan. Have a clear start, middle and finish to a lesson. Organise prior to the lesson to ensure everything is to hand. Use assertive delivery. Gain pupil attention before giving the next instruction. Refer to the previous task so pupils see the link between tasks. Arrange furniture to suit the activity. Use recap – activity – recap.
Show enthusiasm	Smile. Focus on the positive aspects of the topic you are teaching. Use encouraging gestures.
Set appropriate challenges	Encourage pupils to go 'one step further'. Always have extension tasks ready and set them in advance (possibly with a menu of activities to work through on the board). Provide a choice of tasks.
Be assertive	Aim to be assertive rather than aggressive. Be decisive, e.g. when setting tasks, choosing pupils to do things, collecting in materials, etc.
Use humour	Use humour appropriately to resolve situations. Ensure that your body language fits with what you are saying (don't smile when you are reprimanding a pupil). Don't be afraid to laugh with the class.
Emphasise the importance of the learning	Keep your focus on the learning. Keep coming back to this as the key issue. Tick your learning objectives off to chart progress through the lesson. Do not get side-tracked by irrelevant questions (be polite, but assertive).
Cut out peripheral chat/ low-level disruption	Do not talk over pupils. Use a click, stare, etc. in the first instance. Use pupils' names to correct individuals. Wait for silence. (And tell them what you are waiting for!) Move pupils who continue to talk. Set up a seating plan if necessary.
Check completion of tasks	Avoid asking if they understand all the time. Try not to constantly ask, 'Have you finished?'. Monitor body language and facial expression to gauge understanding.
Avoid confrontation	Focus on the ground rules and reasons for them. Don't get into arguments. Don't punish whole classes. Give pupils a chance to 'put things right'/make amends.

Perhaps the trainee teacher simply does not understand how to demonstrate that she is addressing the target. This may be because the target is vague, or because there is a lack of negotiated strategies. In this case, the mentor's role is to clarify the target and exemplify some strategies, perhaps with examples from her own or others' practice, as we described earlier. This could involve the trainee in some targeted observation and the mentor in some explicit modelling of a particular strategy.

Alternatively, the trainee teacher might not acknowledge the issue, or think that he knows better. He may be discounting the problem (see Chapter 5). If a trainee teacher disagrees with the feedback given, or challenges the strategies being suggested, a mentor may need to give him the freedom to try his own ideas. Sometimes, this can lead to the target being addressed in a way not anticipated by the mentor – or, alternatively, it can lead to a trainee acknowledging that the mentor knows best!

Of course, it might be that the trainee is not capable of meeting the target or of acting upon advice and feedback. This does happen, and it is at this point that the conversation might need to be about whether she is enjoying teaching. Teaching is not for everyone, and a mentor may need to support a trainee in recognising this. Most trainee teachers are motivated and driven to be successful. They want to be teachers and are amenable to ideas and feedback. The profession demands that teachers are open to innovation, coaching and mentoring. Pointing this out might be what is required to support the trainee teacher to recognise that it is a role that he will not enjoy. Most trainee teachers will not need these prompts, and, if this is the appropriate conclusion, they will reach it independently. On the rare occasions that a trainee teacher does not acknowledge this, a mentor will need to guide him by candidly discussing his capability and motivation to continue.

As a brilliant mentor, your key role of observing trainee teachers teaching and giving formative developmental feedback drives the development of practice. The nature of observation and its importance in securing trainee teachers' progress are paramount in the development of the mentoring conversation. As Mike Hughes (1999) said, 'The biggest and most underused resource teachers have is each other'.

References

General Teaching Council for England (2004) *The learning conversation*, London: GTC.

Howell, W. S. (1982) *The empathic communicator*, University of Minnesota: Wadsworth Publishing Company.

Hughes, M. (1999) *Closing the learning gap*, 1st edition, Stafford: Network Educational Press.

Vygotsky, L. S. (1986) *Thought and language*, trans. and ed. A. Kozulen, Cambridge, MA: MIT Press.

Chapter 5

Emotional intelligence

Sandra Newell and Shaun Hughes

There are at least two realities for us as teachers – the objective and the subjective. The *objective* is our experience of the external world as we live it – the systems, the timetables, the processes – our day-to-day, minute-by-minute existence. This includes the countless interactions between us and our pupils – the everyday business of the busy school.

The *subjective* concerns how we experience all of this individually, and how it makes us feel. What range of emotions do we go through in a typical day? And how does this affect how we feel, our performance, our motivation, our health and our well-being?

In this chapter, we want to consider the relationship between the objective and the subjective, and how this affects us as teachers, trainees and mentors. For example: how do I judge whether I've had a good day at work? Does this relate to completing all the tasks I set myself, and maintaining a smooth and effective classroom? Or does it really concern how positive and happy I feel about my experiences? Of course, the two are intimately connected, but the mentor needs to be aware of them both and of their mutual impact.

One new teacher teaches an excellent lesson but is overly self-critical afterwards, focusing on the negative aspects and dismissing the praise. Another trainee is too confident and believes that his unsatisfactory lesson is good. He does not act on advice to improve it. How does a mentor attempt to understand the subjective realities of new teachers? How do the mentor and new teacher develop shared meaning? How does the mentor ensure that she hears what the new teacher says and does not impose her own meaning on it? One of the roles of a mentor is to have clear, objective criteria for evaluating teaching, and to be aware of the new teacher's subjectivity and the need to develop a relationship in which objectivity and trust can be fostered.

Relationships with other people are at the core of everything we are and everything we do. They are fundamental to success in many areas, including education. Good relationships are at the heart of good learning, and the mentoring relationship is no exception. But what makes good relationships, and what causes relationships to break down?

The relationship between the mentor and the trainee is a very special one. It requires awareness, understanding and empathy, along with a willingness to change. It can awaken feelings, including some that have long been buried and that may come back to the surface as a result of verbal exchanges, which can sometimes be uncomfortable.

Emotional intelligence

Mentors are both role models and leaders within these dialogues, and this complex role depends upon emotional intelligence. There is an *unspoken emotional dimension* to leadership. If a leader has emotional intelligence, it tends to be mimicked by others within the hierarchy, and so it sets a productive emotional climate in which to work.

A key role of a mentor is to support the new teacher in a variety of ways. She gives emotional support, as well as informational support and instrumental support (House 1981).

So, what is 'emotional intelligence'? According to Goleman (1996), there are five key elements to the Emotional Quotient (EQ). The first is *self–awareness*. People with this quality recognise their feelings as they happen; they understand their emotions, but they don't let their feelings rule them. They are confident and in control. They are willing to take an honest look at themselves. They know their strengths and weaknesses and they want to work on them so they can perform better. A mentor who has self-awareness is likely to understand what is happening in the mentoring conversation and during feedback. This is the first step to developing a good relationship with the new teacher.

Second, there is *self-regulation*. People can manage their emotions. They have the ability to control their emotions and impulses. They think before they act. They rarely become angry or jealous, and they don't make impulsive or careless decisions. They are thoughtful and comfortable with change. They have integrity, and sufficient assertiveness to say 'no'. They can bounce back quickly from setbacks and disappointments. These qualities would empower the mentor and new teacher to monitor what is happening and respond appropriately.

The third element is *motivation*. People with a high EQ are usually motivated. They can delay gratification. They tend to be highly productive, love a challenge and are very effective in every-thing they do. In an ideal world, mentors become mentors and new teachers want to be teachers because they are highly motivated and relish the challenge involved. It is likely that a motivated mentor is reading this book!

Empathy is the fourth element. People with a high EQ are empathetic. This is the ability to identify with, and understand, the wants, needs and viewpoints of those around them. They can recognise the feelings of others, even when these are not especially obvious. This means that they are excellent at managing relation-ships, listening and relating to others. They avoid stereotyping and judging too quickly, and they live their lives in a very open and honest way. These people tend to do well in the caring professions. This is a highly desirable skill for a mentor.

Finally, emotional intelligence requires *social skills*. People with high EQ have high social skills and can get on with people. They are easy to talk to, and concerned with others rather than with themselves. They can manage disputes, are excellent communicators and are masters at building and maintaining relationships. They also tend to be popular and make good leaders.

The understanding of these key features of emotional intelligence – self-awareness, self-regulation, motivation, empathy and social skills – is essential for mentors to fully support their trainees. The exploration of these components or facets by both the mentor and trainee not only strengthens the mentoring relationship, but also establishes a strong foundation for learning and for the development of a successful teacher.

Successful new teachers develop in their skills of teaching, but also in their emotional intelligence and their understanding of how learning is affected by the emotions. It is important to be able to persist in the face of difficulty and to get along with colleagues. Their acceptance of themselves and their ability to form professional working relationships that are warm and positive are signs of good emotional intelligence. They grow in their autonomy over the period of their training. They develop a sense of mastery over their circumstances.

Transactional analysis – the drivers

The idea that grown-up life patterns are affected by childhood experiences is a common one in psychology. Transactional Analysis (TA) suggests the concept of *drivers*, of which there are five: *Be Perfect, Please Others, Try Hard, Be Strong* and *Hurry Up*, each of which has a distinctive set of words, tones, gestures, postures and facial expressions (Kahler 1974, in Stewart and Joines 1987). These can be present in everyone but, within any individual, one or two may dominate. There are speculations as to the origins of these drivers. Some people think they might be partly inborn, others see them as survival strategies for the baby.

These drivers (so called because we feel a compulsion to follow them) are also the results of behaviour that is encouraged by parents or carers, whether verbally or otherwise. They become our strengths and our weaknesses. They are intimately connected with attitudes to change. In the mentoring relationship, these drivers might demonstrate themselves in a variety of ways:

The *mentor* who has a *Be Perfect* driver will set very high standards for her new teacher; she may be overly critical and is likely to want to rewrite her observation forms 'in best'. The *new teacher* who has this driver will work until very late, redo work until it is 'perfect' and be very self-critical.

The *mentor* who strives to *Please Others* will want to ensure that feedback is well received; she will worry about offering negative comments or criticising the new teacher's lesson. She is likely to keep asking the new teacher if everything is all right. A *new teacher* with this driver will over-adapt to the mentor's way of doing things and constantly seek reassurance.

With a *Try Hard* driver, the *mentor* and *new teacher* will actually use the word 'try' repeatedly. When asked, for example, to set more focused and measurable learning objectives, the new teacher may say, 'I tried to . . .', or 'I am trying to be focused', or 'I will try . . .'. Sometimes, *trying* replaces *doing* in these exchanges.

The *Be Strong mentor* will appear matter-of-fact and lacking in emotion. She may display closed body language and use distancing techniques, believing that 'teachers must not show weaknesses' – by which she means that 'I must not show weaknesses'. Although hurt or upset by critical feedback, the *new teacher* will brush it off when asked how she feels, saying 'I'm fine, I like criticism; it forces me to improve'.

As you might expect, the *mentor* with a *Hurry Up* driver will rush feedback and trainee meetings and will hurry the new teacher when he is evaluating his lesson. She may well interrupt. She will appear agitated. The *new teacher* with this driver will be impatient to receive his feedback and will struggle to wait for a planned meeting to discuss issues. He may allow his anxiety to override rational courtesies or protocols.

If mentors are aware of these drivers, they can intervene to help new teachers develop in a supportive atmosphere. For each of these drivers, there is an antidote, known as an *allower*, and it may be the mentor's job to find the allower in herself and in her trainee. If a mentor has a new teacher with a *Be Perfect* driver, she needs to encourage him to replace the critical internal voice with something like, 'I have done my best. This is good enough. It is OK for me to have a rest now.'

For *Please Others*, the allower is 'please yourself' – ensure you get your own needs met as well as meeting those of others. For *Try Hard*, the mentor response might be, 'Don't try . . . *do* it'. For *Be Strong*, the mentor should encourage the new teacher to express his feelings; and, as we might expect, for *Hurry Up*, the trainee should be told, 'take your time'. All of these correctives need to be offered gently and with positive encouragement, rather than critically or aggressively. These allowers can be used like affirmations. The new teacher can repeat his allower to himself (like a mantra) or even write it on a sticky note in a prominent position. At first, this may feel uncomfortable, as he may be trying to undo years of conditioning and practice.

Drivers can prevent contact with the present. People can be lost in their subjective world. Take the moment when a new teacher is given some feedback that involves criticism, whether implied or overt. This can 'rubber band' the recipient back to a time when she first felt this way. She may even subconsciously visualise the individual (usually a family member) who criticised her originally. This is known as *transference* and is particularly common in relationships where there is a power imbalance, as the original critic is often a parent figure.

The key to good relationships is to interact with people in the present, to monitor thoughts, feelings and behaviour, and respond appropriately.

The Drama Triangle

Mentors (and new teachers) will also benefit from knowing about the *Drama Triangle*, as devised by Stephen Karpman (1968). This is another example of how emotional intelligence and immediacy can be sabotaged. The three roles in this are those of *Persecutor*, *Rescuer* and *Victim*. The *Persecutor* dominates and criticises; the *Rescuer* offers help, often giving more help than is needed, and the *Victim* seeks help, feeling that he cannot cope on his own. In the Drama Triangle, a person may start off in one of the three positions and gradually move into the other two. Each of these roles is likely to compromise reality and progress.

Let us look at a concrete example in a mentoring relationship that is not working effectively. The mentor gives the new teacher the feedback that his planning is poor and needs to be improved (thus acting as *Persecutor*). The new teacher tells the mentor that he was up until 2 o'clock in the morning planning and does not know how to improve; he thinks that perhaps he is not cut out for teaching and asks the mentor to help him (adopting the role of *Victim*). The mentor then offers to plan the lesson for the new teacher (becoming the *Rescuer*). The new teacher then teaches the lesson, and it still does not go well. The new teacher then blames the mentor for having planned the lesson in such a way that he could not deliver it in his own style (switching to *Persecutor*) – and so it goes on. One way of recognising whether a mentor is playing (or overplaying) the part of the Rescuer is for her to ask herself how much of the task she is taking on. If it is more than 50 per cent, then it is likely that she is playing the Rescuer. She might instead sit down with the new teacher and go through the planning of a lesson, asking questions to elicit the ideas from him, instead of doing it for him.

Discounting

In all of these roles, there is an element of *discounting* (Mellor and Sigmund 1975, in Stewart and Joines 1987). This is when a person unconsciously ignores information that might help him to solve a problem. When we have a problem, we have two options. We can use our adult thinking to solve it, or we can go into what is sometimes known as our *script* – the version of our lives that we have created and followed since childhood. If we do this, instead of taking action to solve the problem, we revert to childhood thinking to try to get someone to find the solution for us.

In fact, there are four types of behaviour that can demonstrate that a person is discounting when there is a problem. These are: *doing nothing, over-adaptation, agitation* and *incapacitation* or *violence*. In mentoring, they may demonstrate themselves in various ways. For example, when asked by a mentor what he might do to solve a particular problem, a trainee remains silent. He uses a passive behaviour in which he discounts his ability to do anything about the situation; so he *does nothing*. Alternatively, when a new teacher *over-adapts*, he complies with what he thinks the mentor wants him to say or do without checking with her. He might try to second-guess what she wants him to say. Again, the new teacher may display *agitation*. He discounts his ability to solve the problem and instead becomes agitated. This might involve a purposeless, repetitive activity, such as tapping a pen or drumming his fingers to redirect the discomfort. Finally, in extreme cases, there may be *incapacitation*. This might involve, for example, becoming ill and even staying at home, in order to avoid a problem instead of solving it. This technique can be seen as *violence* directed inwards. Other violent behaviour may be directed towards objects – such as slamming a folder down or hitting a wall. The new teacher releases a burst of energy that might be directed against himself, other people or objects to try to force the environment to solve the problem for him.

There are three *areas* that a person can discount. These are the self, other people and the situation. There are also three *types* of discounting: stimuli, options and problems. When a person discounts a stimulus, she discounts the fact that there is a problem at all, or she may realise that there is a problem but discount the fact that there are options available to solve it. Finally, there are four *levels* of discounting: discounting the *existence* of a problem; discounting the *significance* of the problem; discounting the fact that there are *possibilities to change* the situation and discounting our own *personal ability* to solve a problem.

Let us come back to our mentor and new teacher. The mentor has given the new teacher some feedback about behavioural problems in the lesson he just taught. The new teacher says that he did not see any behaviour issues in the lesson (discounting their *existence*). The mentor goes on to tell him that there might be health and safety issues involved with the pupils' misbehaviour. The trainee replies that it really wasn't that serious, that the pupils were just having a laugh (discounting the *significance*). She then asks him how he might improve the situation, and he says that he does not think he can (discounting *the possibility of change*). Finally, she asks what he can do about his body language and voice in order to improve his behaviour-management skills, and he says he doesn't think there is anything he can do (discounting his *personal ability* to solve the problem).

So, what can a mentor do when she notices a new teacher discounting? The first thing is to have the awareness in order to notice the discount and pick it up. The second step is to (gently) challenge the discount; and the third step is to point the person to ways in which he might be able to solve the problem himself.

Accentuate the positive

When new teachers are training, they often comment on the number of targets they are set on a daily basis. These may be set by their mentors or by various teachers to whom they are attached throughout the day. Occasionally, they become overwhelmed by negativity and fail to notice the positive comments that are made to them as well. Sometimes, they need to be encouraged to take note of the positive feedback as well as the suggestions for improvement. It is up to the mentor too to ensure that she gives genuine, positive feedback. *Positive Psychology*, which focuses on what goes right in life (Peterson 2006), encourages people to look at strengths, show gratitude and have hope. In a mentoring relationship, this means ensuring that the mentor points out the new teacher's strengths, verbalises gratitude for the hard work that he has done, and expresses clear belief that he can continue to improve.

Although the mentor is probably not a trained counsellor, and her role is not to counsel the new teacher on personal matters, some of the skills involved in counselling are powerful when used in the mentoring relationship. Good listening, for example, involves good eye contact, not interrupting and not being distracted – which can sometimes be a challenge in a busy school day. Paraphrasing and summarising what has been said by the new teacher – communicating briefly what he has said, using 'so . . .' – is a good way of confirming and clarifying issues. Advanced empathy, in which the mentor shows that she has perceived what the person is feeling and articulates what has been implied, as well as what has actually been said, is an important skill. The clues here may come from the body language.

One very useful counselling intervention that mentors can use is that of *immediacy*. This means expressing immediately and explicitly what is happening. For example, if a mentor notices that every time she gives advice to a new teacher it is met with the words 'Yes, but . . .', she could draw the new teacher's attention to the fact that this is happening. This clearly needs to be done in a non-confrontational way. 'I notice that, every time I make a suggestion, you say, "Yes, but . . ." I wonder whether you might respond differently, or just say "Yes".' If it happens again, the mentor could gently remind the new teacher that this is recurring: 'I am aware that whenever I give you positive feedback, you immediately discount it or dismiss it. What is going on for you at that point?'. This type of intervention is useful too with body language: 'I notice that when I mention something positive about your lesson, you look away. Have you any ideas what that might be about?'.

The power of language and the way it is delivered in a mentoring relationship cannot be underestimated. Many new teachers, for example, say that their mentor talks to them 'like one of the pupils'. Mentors can respond to new teachers in a variety of ways. If, for example, the new teacher has just taught a very good lesson, the mentor may use:

- the *active–constructive* response, which is enthusiastic – 'That was a great lesson, well done . . .'
- the *active–destructive* response, which points out the potential downside – 'I'll expect this standard in all your lessons from now on . . .'
- the *passive–constructive* response, which is muted – 'That was quite good . . .'
- the *passive–destructive* response, which conveys lack of interest – 'I've got to go to a meeting now . . .'

Relationships are more likely to flourish if active–constructive responses are used when something good happens (Gable *et al.* 2004).

The culture of the school

An important consideration with all of the psychological theories that underpin effective personal and working relationships is the prevailing culture of the school and how open teachers are to this kind of professional dialogue.

Schools are interpenetrating worlds. We all participate in the physical world, while at the same time having a rich thought-life and continuous self-talk, informed by and reacting to our experiences and emotional intelligence. We all have our mental models. These are our assumptions, our understanding of how our world works, and they are hugely influential in helping us understand the world. Some of these models are fixed and rarely challenged. They form a complex web of experience and learning, developed from early childhood. At the same time, we are continually constructing our mental models in response to our own existence and our complex and multiple interactions.

Let us consider two individuals, John and Susie, working together in this maelstrom of activity that is school life. The school is not only a machine-like organisation but has a complex mix of subjective and objective experience built on the interactions of many people, all with their own mental models and, to some degree, expressing their own mental worlds, driven by a wide range of drivers, some conscious, some unconscious.

John has a clear view of himself; he is confident and happy. His model of the world and his place in it have been confirmed and validated by his friends and family. He is an only child and has the feeling that, if he thinks, feels and believes something, then others will concur. He has never had to negotiate with siblings. Occasionally, since he decided to train as a teacher, his self-talk or inner voice has been heard quietly raising doubts, but he has not paid too much attention. In his previous work in business, John was well within his comfort zone. He knew what he had to do. He had many experiences of success, which gave him confidence and a strong sense of self-efficacy. He knew everyone and he knew how the systems and processes worked. Moving out of his comfort zone has been harder than he thought. At the same time, however, he has relished the challenge, the exposure to new ideas and new learning. His most dominant driver is *Be Strong*: he will not give way to feelings. When he is troubled, he will keep this to himself. *Be Strong* people will make reliable workers. They will keep their feelings at a distance from themselves and other people, but they tend to be poor communicators, and either don't recognise difficulties or are afraid of them being found out.

Susie similarly is successful and happy, although for her there is more questioning and a niggling doubt that somehow life could have been different, and that something is missing. She comes from a large family and has a highly intelligent, dominant older sister. She has always felt in her shadow to some extent and has struggled to be heard. Despite achieving highly herself, she has a sense of 'could do better'. This was confirmed by a rather aggressive and authoritarian father. She is, however, an excellent teacher, with a big heart. At school she feels in control; she feels that she is supported by the school and totally comfortable with its systems. She is very well respected by other teachers. She knows her job, she can understand and motivate her pupils and get good results.

The two of them come together in a professional relationship – Susie as mentor, John as trainee. Susie has been a mentor for several years. She has felt challenged in this role before, especially by men, and is well aware that this may have something to do with her father. She is aware of herself and has been working to understand her feelings and responses. She has a strong sense of being a professional and a robust self-efficacy in these areas. She has an intuitive understanding that what she is learning from her mentoring work is valuable for herself. She has a good understanding of herself, although this is not complete. For her, mentoring is not just about helping the students to meet the required standards; it is more a shared journey of discovery.

John and Susie are going to challenge each other in quite different ways. This isn't going to be a master/apprentice relationship; it is much more complex than this. It is going to be a 'helping relationship', and it will take its course in a developmental space.

The development space is the learning for both of them. The relationship is not emotionally neutral. Subjective and objective experiences are going to be explored, and it is this that will give the mentoring and coaching their transformational power.

Susie is aware that the first stage will involve her attending to John's emotional intelligence. How aware is he of himself, and how sensitive does he seem to others? This is important for Susie. How does John relate to the pupils? What are his core values and beliefs around teaching, and how well formed are they? How does he relate to her as his mentor? How does he respond to criticism? Will he listen? For Susie, these early stages will be about understanding John. Where and what is his centre of gravity? She will do her best, knowing that a good relationship is important for the mentoring that lies ahead.

Susie is up for it. Somewhere deep inside herself she recognises that this experience of helping others is what she needs and enjoys. It helps her grow and develop. She is very aware that the map is not the territory, and that they will both learn new things. The period of training is laid out before them both, the timetable is clear, the standards, the observations, the feedback, the dialogue, are all clear. The journey, though, is unknown and, to some extent, unpredictable.

However, John, at this stage, is blissfully unaware of what he is about to go through. He is full of confidence and is not expecting too much trouble. He is confident in his subject knowledge, confident that he can meet the challenges ahead. He has not failed so far.

Through the window

In considering these people and their blind spots, we might use the Johari windows as a framework for exploring communication and understanding. There are four metaphorical windows: the *public*, the *hidden*, the *blind* and the *unknown*.

A great deal is known already about John and Susie – who they are, what their roles are, their reputations. This is all in the *public* domain. As their relationship develops, they may or may not decide to reveal more. As trust grows, and they feel more comfortable with each other, this may well happen naturally. They may reveal personal or professional matters. This is the *hidden* window. The degree of revelation may well be in proportion to the trust and rapport that is built up between them. Another window exists within which will be all that they will learn about each other, but will be wary to communicate. It may be that John will think Susie too critical or lacking in humour; and it may be that Susie will see John as rather arrogant and overconfident. Each may see irritating habits in the other. Body language may be a problem. In general, these issues and reactions tend to remain hidden and unspoken, unless, of course, they become significant professional factors. It's what other people know about you but they don't tell you. This is the *blind* window.

The final window in this model is perhaps the most fascinating. No one knows what is contained here. This has the greatest potential for learning and growth. John doesn't know what he is capable of, and neither does Susie. In some ways, all mentoring and coaching can be seen as shining a light into this space. This is the *unknown* window.

The mentoring and coaching processes run their course, and issues are steered around, confronted, ignored or encompassed within this unfolding relationship. A great deal of learning goes on. The skills of teaching are developed, new teachers are inculcated into the profession, and understanding of how to work with children, young people and adults is arrived at or worked towards. Robust systems of lesson planning, observation and feedback are followed. Judgements are moderated. However, beneath this, another kind of learning is happening. This is personal and is to do with responding to challenge and deep learning. It is partly this duality that makes training to teach simultaneously exhilarating and exhausting.

Teachers need to know themselves very well indeed in order to cope, but also in order to teach and to help. John and Susie will know themselves well, but teaching and the mentoring relationship will intensify and challenge this process. John's behaviour will be informed by his life so far. This behaviour will be based on some beliefs that may well be out of date. These may be habit or defence mechanisms of some kind. His reaction to any incident will be determined by this complex mix of influences. Let's consider one such incident during John's teaching placement.

Early on in the practice, there was a problem with a group of girls. They approached Susie to say that they felt John was rude to them and talked down to them, and that he was more interested in the boys. He had also made some comment about their hair, which they didn't like.

John had no idea this was a problem. Susie did: she had observed that he rarely asked any of the girls a question, ignored them for much of the time, and certainly enjoyed banter with the 'lads'. John was behaving as he always had. He was a little sexist; had had very little to do with girls. He had been spoiled by his mother. He believed that girls liked being talked to in a particular way and enjoyed comments about their hair. When this was raised, he at first resisted the criticism and became defensive.

Susie's role here was to broach this issue, not in a judgemental way, but in order to raise awareness and to explore John's mental model. John's reaction when this blind spot is revealed will say much about his current emotional intelligence and the way he handles criticism. Not only does he have to come to realisation that this is the current reality, but he has to learn from it, change his behaviour and move on. He will also need to provide evidence that things have changed and, moreover, to repair the damaged relationship with the girls. These kinds of issue will continually arise, especially in the early years of teaching, and it is here that the role of the mentor is so vital. How Susie manages this situation will affect the future mentoring relationship but also the relationship with the pupils. Issues in the early years are sometimes about subject knowledge, but more often than not are about the relationships with pupils and colleagues.

Susie is also challenged by this. She will find this difficult, and it will bother her. She may even dwell upon it the night before. There is no doubt that she knows what needs to be done. But, while this may give her courage, she will still find it troublesome. This particular issue will revisit unconscious thoughts from Susie's past and will possibly involve issues of transference or counter-transference. She sometimes finds it difficult to say things that may seem critical. She knows that these thoughts are irrational and has found ways of dealing with them.

John and Susie will continue this dance of mentoring throughout the relationship. Part of this is about the mechanics of teaching. Mentoring involves supporting training and development and constitutes significant investment in time, energy and understanding; but underlying this is reflection and professional dialogue about these important issues of emotional intelligence.

Schools are emotional learning environments, as well as intellectual ones. Emotional well-being is an important factor in successful schools, for both pupils and staff. A great deal of effort is made by schools to establish positive learning environments, but factors such as systems that can seem authoritarian, or behaviour management policies based on punishments and threats, highlight the need for high emotional intelligence on the part of pupils and staff. The ability to perceive, identify and manage emotions provides the basis for a wide range of social and emotional competencies that are important for teachers. An alertness to, and conscious discussion of, emotional intelligence can be seen therefore, not only as supporting new teachers through the challenges of training to teach, but also as means towards establishing emotionally intelligent schools.

References

Gable, S. L., Reis, H. T., Impett, E. A. and Asher, E. R. (2004) 'What do you do when things go right? The intrapersonal and interpersonal benefits of sharing good events', *Journal of Personal and Social Psychology*, 87: 228–45.

Goleman, D. (1996) *Emotional intelligence: why it can matter more than IQ*, London: Bloomsbury.

House, J. S. (1981) *Work stress and social support*, Reading, MA: Addison-Wesley.

Kahler, T. and Capers, H. (1974) 'The miniscript', *Transactional Analysis Journal*, 4(1): 26–42.

Karpman, S. (1968) 'Fairy tales and script drama analysis', *Transactional Analysis Bulletin*, 7(26): 39–43.

Mellor, K. and Sigmund, E. (1975) 'Discounting', *Transactional Analysis Journal*, 5(3): 295–302.

Peterson, C. (2006) *A primer in positive psychology*, New York: Oxford University Press.

Stewart, I. and Joines, V. (1987) *TA today: a new introduction to transactional analysis*, Nottingham: Lifespace Publishing.

Chapter 6

Mentoring together

Paul Clarke

Like teaching, mentoring need not be a solitary business. Just as teachers need to collaborate, mentors may work together to support trainees. This chapter is for people who are working in a subject department where trainees are assigned and where they may teach under the guidance of several different teachers. It explores the creative force behind a *mentoring department,* and how trainees may be helped (and sometimes hindered) by teacher mentors with very different ways of working. It looks at the benefits of spreading the mentoring load between experienced and less experienced teachers, and how the process of mentoring can have an impact on the development of the department.

Most secondary teachers use a subject department as a reference point for thinking about their work. Department colleagues act as role models and as sources for inspiration, reflection and criticism on matters central to day-to-day teaching and learning. It seems sensible, therefore, to think of your department as a base for good *mentoring.* You can argue that there is strength in numbers, and that if you can't think of a solution for a trainee's problem, then you will know someone who can. It is also likely that somewhere, in a department of teachers with different styles and personalities, will be the guidance most suited to a particular trainee teacher. Why assume that a single mentor will be the best source for a trainee in every circumstance throughout the whole of a placement? And, if an imaginative trainee brings a number of new ideas with her, isn't there a case for sharing the experience with as many teachers in the department as is possible?

What is a mentoring department?

The ideal mentoring department is one where every teacher has had mentor training and the experience of working with trainees, where a trainee can draw on the range of staff experience across the department on a regular basis, and where the whole of the department benefits from the presence of the trainee and the dialogue that goes with mentoring. In practice, it is helpful to think of a brilliant department where the culture is one that welcomes trainee teachers and actively courts their participation in every facet of department work. You might be carrying out the role of lead mentor this year, but several of your colleagues would have mentored in previous years and would be willing to share their classes with a trainee to provide a good and varied timetable. Your colleagues would enjoy sharing conversations with you and your trainee about training targets and professional progress. Your role would have been carefully considered as part of the department's development plan.

In such a department, a trainee teacher joins a culture where the expectations are of collaboration, mutual support and an openness in tackling problems. We have discussed collaborative mentoring in a number of earlier chapters, and coaching is the main theme of Chapter 7. The job of welcoming a trainee and creating a workable timetable is one that you might lead as active mentor, but to which others would contribute willingly. There would be advice on routines and resources on hand from whoever was available at the time. The trainee's timetable would involve teaching a range of classes belonging to several different staff, and there would be the opportunity to mix and match classes during a placement to suit the trainee's needs.

While a formal mentor meeting between you and your trainee would be scheduled, the trainee might raise an issue of behaviour management informally over coffee and receive several different ideas from colleagues who have quite different approaches. Colleagues would be used to differences in viewpoints and be interested in the perspective of a relative newcomer to the department. A teaching assistant who works regularly with a difficult pupil might offer very particular kinds of advice, and a meeting to discuss further ideas could be set up without too much difficulty.

In such a mentoring department, the job of planning lessons becomes less troublesome, particularly where specialist subject knowledge is an issue. A trainee can seek advice from those most able to help, and this relieves a considerable burden on an individual mentor. In a department where particular teaching modules are prepared by individuals and then shared as a matter of course between colleagues, a trainee can tap into the good day-to-day practice of the department without seeming to be a burden or doing anything out of the ordinary. Likewise, the time-consuming task for one mentor of observing a whole set of a trainee's lessons can be less irksome when shared between colleagues. Your job then becomes one of helping a trainee to make a sensible synthesis from a potentially rich and varied collection of observation reports, and, as we said in Chapter 2, this synthesising can become a powerful feature of the trainee's dynamic reflection.

A brilliant mentoring department sits comfortably within the culture of collaboration, mentoring and training expected of contemporary schools. It assumes that everyone can (and will) contribute to each other's professional development in a variety of ways. A trainee's naïve questions and ideas can be an important trigger to rethinking a classroom approach for even the most experienced mentor. The more staff are involved in such processes across the department, then the more thoughtful the department's work in general is likely to be. It is but a small step for such a department to accommodate the observation and sharing of practice that has become a common form of school-based training process. There can be a seamless development from classroom reflection and discussion, stemming from the needs of a trainee, to a more widespread debate about effective teaching in a department meeting, and on to a school improvement programme engaging several departments in working and researching together.

A diversity of experience centred on trust

Viewed from the trainee's perspective, the success of the placement in the school and in the particular department rests on the relationship with you as a mentor. Extending the mentoring role to the whole department requires a degree of trust between the trainee and other staff, and, as lead mentor, you have to manage this. This is not always easy and takes time to establish. An important idea is to think of how your role of lead mentor in a department might change during a placement. At the beginning, a trainee is likely to spend most of the time under your wing, and an induction period could be based around observation and shared work with your own classes. The initial conversations, which help to establish confidence and shared expectations for teaching and learning, are with you, though there may be some limited observation of other colleagues' teaching that you discuss together.

When the trainee is ready for a teaching experience, you could include lessons with another colleague and arrange time to plan and review these together with them. You might choose to work with a colleague who has a different approach, for example in the management of pupils' practical work, and set out to explore these differences as an explicit part of a mentor meeting. Care taken at this stage should help to prepare your trainee to work with others in the department in the same way for the remainder of the placement.

At a later point, your trainee could take on a wider range of classes, working with a larger number of staff. Some departments have helped to make this whole process 'public' by using a noticeboard in the office to share developments, with the trainee's approval. The trainee's presence is seen as an important part of the department's agenda, and the responsibilities are seen to be shared. Behind the scenes, you would need to be checking that colleagues are managing the feedback process successfully and that any of their concerns are taken forward into your formal mentor meeting.

The trainee is now experiencing the best of what the department can offer, both in terms of quality and diversity. Diversity may be a matter of different subject specialisms, different perspectives on issues such as behaviour management or perhaps varied reflections of colleagues' experience.

In one relatively small business department, a head of department with twenty years' teaching and mentoring experience was able to oversee the trainee's collaborative work with three other members of staff, each of whom offered something special. A mature business manager who had pursued teaching as a second career had a rich fund of business anecdotes and a real sense of business leadership, which was highly valued by older pupils. His serious tone and no-nonsense class management approach were impressive to observe but difficult to adopt by a new, young trainee teacher. A younger teacher used humour and a wealth of local knowledge, as well as her relationships as an assistant year head, to engage younger pupils in a variety of lively activities. The fun in her classroom was obvious, but the strong relationships and knowledge of individual pupils that underpinned her work were less explicit to the untrained eye. The fourth member of the department had just completed her year as a newly qualified teacher (NQT) and was very aware of the trials and tribulations faced by the trainee.

All were interested in working with the trainee, and the head of department, acting as lead mentor, was able to draw each person in turn into a form of mentoring that served the trainee well. Carefully managed observations and discussion allowed the trainee to see the value of business examples to aid pupil learning, without having to feel intimidated by the strong classroom presence of that particular teacher. When the trainee was feeling a little downhearted after a particularly difficult lesson, the newly qualified teacher was able to provide positive support in language and pitch entirely in tune with the needs of a raw beginner. The sense that there is light at the end of the training tunnel can seem more understandable and credible coming from a recent recruit than from the more seasoned mentor. The teacher who doubled up her department commitments with a pastoral role provided a helpful department–school balance to the conversation. Her insights were often drawn from contact with pupils and staff outside the department, and she opened a door to the whole school and encouraged the trainee to look outside a subject classroom for inspiration.

It would not be hard for a casual visitor to pick up on the very positive and open environment in which this department works. A shared office space ensures regular contact on both a formal and informal basis. Resources and laptops are to hand, as are coffee-making facilities. Someone is likely to come in and share her delights and frustrations about an activity that has been tried out for the first time. Everyone can be seen to be having good moments and bad, to be expressing feelings as well as more measured professional judgements, and this provides a legitimacy for a trainee to try out the same. Conversations about lesson plans, pupil activities, good questions to start and finish a lesson, are the remit of *everyone* and not just a mentor huddled in a corner of the staffroom with a trainee.

Through skilled mediation and careful protection of people's time, the head of department, acting as lead mentor, engaged everyone in activities that played to their individual strengths and yet also met the needs of the trainee. The sum of the experience would probably be beyond the talents of any one mentor. The discussion in the department office focused on the trainee's progress, but also reminded department members of their relative strengths and of how they could continue to learn from each other. It would be entirely reasonable to picture the role of lead mentor to be interchangeable between members of this department in the next two or three years.

Some potential pitfalls

It is not hard to think of some of the very real difficulties involved in moving towards department mentoring. Trusting relationships need to exist between members of a department themselves before they can be modelled for a trainee teacher. A department with a strong hierarchical management style is likely to find it difficult to embrace the give-and-take conversations described in the business department example above. The separation of responsibilities as a head of department and as a lead mentor can also create friction.

A lead mentor may need to ask for the particular support of a member of staff on behalf of a trainee, and this may not come easily if this is seen to usurp the authority of a head of department. Some time in a department meeting may be needed for trainee business, and this may be difficult in a large department with many administrative needs to attend to. A department with a staff-recruitment problem or a struggling colleague would not want to extend the mentoring responsibilities beyond a small number of committed staff.

Anyone who takes on a mentoring role needs to be doing it for positive reasons, and not because he or she has been told to do so by a line manager. There are some people who are good teachers of pupils but less successful as teachers of adults. Earlier chapters have spelled out the expectations and skills required of brilliant mentors, and it is unlikely that a department will be brilliant at mentoring when some of its staff are reluctant participants.

Of course, a small department may only have one or two staff, and taking on a trainee may well require departmental mentoring, but without the diverse resources and experiences that so benefit a trainee in a larger department. Clearly, the benefits of buddying-up with other departments to share mentoring experiences can help, and some small departments seek the shelter and resources of larger faculty structures for mentoring purposes. Small departments may also have small physical spaces in which to operate, leaving trainees little or no room in which to experience the collaborative workspace described earlier. Some schools have a shared room where trainees can work together, but this can move the training culture from the department to elsewhere in the school.

Perhaps the most common concern is about effective communication. Trainee teachers can find it difficult enough to understand exactly what is expected of them when working with *one* dedicated mentor. When day-to-day contact about lesson planning, teaching and assessment is with *several* teaching staff, then problems can multiply. What paperwork is expected and when? Does every member of the department have the same expectations about the documentation required for a well-planned lesson? How far in advance do outlines and details need to be seen? Is it reasonable to communicate by email rather than seek out face-to-face discussions? What about feedback on lesson observations? Is it your role as lead mentor to carry these out to ensure consistency? Should the completion of such forms be the subject matter of a departmental meeting or an extra meeting for everyone concerned?

What if the feedback is different between staff? One teacher requests the trainee to get tough on behaviour management, while two others recommend the use of fewer sanctions and more rewards. How do these kinds of comment become reconciled through your weekly meeting as lead mentor?

It is likely that you would want to talk through such issues with the staff concerned at the early stages of a placement, or before its beginning. Some departments have found it helpful to use a dedicated department meeting to discuss these issues and generate their own set of guidelines as a result, before the arrival of trainees. You may want to lead such a discussion, or even use a senior mentor in the school to support and prompt at the meeting. Such discussions are likely to be of great benefit to the department in all of its work.

It is certainly the case that communication with university tutors or senior staff in school would need to be channelled through you. Issues requiring a coordinated response, such as visit arrangements for tutors or the completion of periodic progress reports, would be your responsibility. Quite simply, the whole mentoring department needs to be well organised and to have effective procedures at departmental level for communicating about, and reporting on, a trainee's progress.

For day-to-day paperwork, the best departments and mentors seem to succeed in creating a culture of 'mediated self-reliance'. The trainee is expected to manage the detail, while the mentor monitors progress through weekly meetings. When an issue about inconsistency arises, your role as lead mentor is to discuss it with the trainee and, when necessary, to mediate between the trainee and other staff.

A common example is the delay in writing lesson observation reports. Trainees may be receiving advice in a good-quality discussion after lessons, often involving several staff and not just the teacher who carried out the observation. However, the formal report

is delayed, even reaching the point where the trainee feels embarrassed to chase the paperwork again.

A confident, self-reliant trainee may feel able to summarise the discussion and send a copy to the teacher for a confirmatory signature. A less confident trainee may need your help to talk with the teacher. Your colleague may enjoy the oral mentoring and may not have understood the need for a trainee to have good-quality written evidence of progress. This is understandably frustrating, and you may well be tempted to think it is simpler to do all this yourself in the first place. If you look on the process as an investment in the department, with yourself as an informal trainer, then the time has been well spent.

There are other issues with big departments, where you are constrained as lead mentor by split sites, by the layout of a single site or by the presence of some part-time staff, all of which can add up to a communication nightmare. In such cases, we would suggest *thinking big about small steps* towards shared mentoring. The successful shared mentoring of a trainee by three colleagues in a department of twelve may be the art of the possible. You may be setting up a role model for things to come.

Another pitfall of mentoring as a department can be in the management of a weak trainee. In the context of a relatively short period in school, a weak trainee needs to be identified at an early stage, and the communication problems described above can be a serious impediment. The support for a trainee in such circumstances needs to be focused and tightly managed. This often involves reducing the scale and complexity of the training activities: for example, by cutting the number of classes being taught and by focusing on a number of quite specific development points. There should be as few ambiguities as is possible, and the trainee should not be in a position to claim that the advice given was in any way contradictory. This all adds up to the need for you, as lead mentor, to be overseeing events as closely as possible and to be setting and monitoring targets. This is not the time to be in the middle of a busy office, nor to be having several different voices playing in the trainee's ear.

There is a case for arguing that, if relationships are good between a weak trainee and several staff in a department, then it can be a good idea to continue the department-mentoring role. If several members of staff are all offering the same kind of professional advice, then a trainee who may be a little thick-skinned and unreceptive, for example, can hear the message loud and clear. It may also be the case that, if your relationship with the trainee is not all that you hoped, then another colleague may establish a stronger link and effect real progress. Some departments have used the television-crime-show analogy of *good cop–bad cop* in describing their preferred approach to a weak trainee. As ever, there are no hard and fast rules, but a brilliant mentoring department needs to be good at picking up and passing the baton, as and when required, and exploiting the diversity of plurality.

What does it take to develop a mentoring department?

It is clear from the example of the business department above that one way to move from mentor to mentoring department is to tackle it in gentle stages. As each new trainee joins a department, so the number of teachers involved in the process is increased. The role of lead mentor could be shared, though this is not always popular with trainees, who often find it confusing. It would be sensible to include any plans for development in the department's formal planning documents and to seek proper time allocations for mentors.

The mentoring experience usually encourages more reflection about good practice in teaching and learning. It requires more conversations between mentors and other staff about the professional training process and a need for the systematic collection of evidence to support judgements about a trainee's progress. It can require imagination, empathy, determination and sensitivity in no small measure. To pass the responsibility between colleagues who have differing degrees of personal skills for mentoring requires planning and good leadership in a department.

It also needs a degree of stability in a department. It is difficult to consider developments of this kind in a department with significant staffing changes, especially at the top level. School reorganisation or major curriculum changes may also preclude a shift in mentoring responsibilities. There is a time and a place for everything.

Some departments have viewed mentoring developments as so important that they have been made the focus of staff training. This has taken the form of a training day supported by university tutors and devoted to mentoring and the principles that underpin good practice. Training materials have been used that focus on the strengths of the department and the ability of staff to support a varied training programme; on the nature of good training programmes; and on how best to plan for progression in trainees' learning. A department that seeks such development would do well to contact training providers with whom it works.

Some departments have been surprised at the extent of their expertise and interests but have found it a challenging task to think how they can be used to meet the national training standards. Attitudes towards trainees and their presence in busy departments have been challenged by thinking how trainees would benefit both the department and individual staff.

Timetabling trainees so that they receive a broad subject experience has usually been the task of a lead mentor. Some good training activities involve the whole department in working on timetabling for prospective trainees, writing constructive feedback reports for trainees based on case study materials and devising action plans for the successful development of trainees in different scenarios.

Finally, some training tasks have asked departments to consider broader issues, such as how they would communicate their plans for mentoring to pupils, to parents and to other colleagues in school. The roles of support teacher, lead mentor and professional mentor in school were explored, as well as resource implication and further training.

Some schools have supported the further development of mentoring through accreditation as part of local university Master's programmes. Groups of mentors have been able to use the products of a year's mentoring and their reflections on the process as the source material for reflective writing. Meetings have been held in schools with the support of visiting university tutors. Again, the important point here is to recognise that the day-to-day mentoring process generates interesting teaching and learning issues that have value over and beyond their immediate context.

One mentor was surprised to find a trainee with creative ideas for teaching maths at a relatively early stage of a placement. He was learning as much, if not more, from his trainee as the trainee was from him. The borderline between mentoring and coaching was blurring. He was also surprised to find this had happened with other department colleagues in previous years and schools, but they had never discussed the issues together. They agreed that the experience was significant in helping them reconsider their own teaching and refresh their professional zeal for the subject. The process of mentoring, of sharing mentoring responsibilities in the department, and finally of talking and writing about these experiences together with a 'critical friend' from university had generated important professional development.

Brilliant mentoring departments can do it differently

A major advantage from working as a mentoring department is the variety of training experiences that can be developed for the benefit of trainees, the department and for training partners. The strength in numbers means that a variety of staff can be involved in many different ways in new kinds of training activity. We have looked so far in this chapter at the collaboration among mentors in whole-mentoring departments. Of course, this may be combined with intensive and structured collaborative working among *trainees* – which we discussed in detail in Chapter 3. For example, one science department, with many years of experience as a training partner with a number of universities, took on *a new way of working with four trainees* studying on a flexible version of the Post-graduate Certificate in Education (PGCE) course. The trainees worked with the department in two different stages: the first as part of an induction into the nature of teaching and learning, and the second as part of an extended first teaching placement. The induction stage involved the group of trainees negotiating some days in school to observe a sequence of lessons and to have some time to discuss the issues at the end of the day. The data they collected served as the basis for further investigation in university and as part of individual study. The second stage involved all four in teaching a 25 per cent timetable, but operating as two pairs. Briefing sessions were provided by different members of the department with different subject knowledge, and trainees were given a 'time allowance' with a range of staff members to manage planning, observation and follow-up discussion. A formal meeting was scheduled with all four trainees and a lead mentor on a weekly basis.

These arrangements were viewed as successful by most participants and prompted a lot of comment about responsibilities for development on the part of the department staff and the trainees.

> *Mentor A*: It's given me the chance to think about my own work; the things I take for granted. It's been less demanding than normal placements because the onus is on the trainee teachers.

I've been involved in their observations of lessons . . . we've given the experiences but they've done the paperwork and have been discussing things together.

Mentor B: It's good in practicals because they can get stuck in. We've had them both in singly and as groups. In one case, we had some special needs pupils who wanted to do a practical. With the group of trainees, in effect we had five teachers and a TA. A fantastic opportunity for pupils and staff.

Mentor C: It seemed a lot for trainee teachers to do on their own; they need to be well on top of normal stuff at an early stage. They needed to be very organised and to have good communication skills to work between themselves, staff and university. It's time consuming because they want to consult all the time.

One mentor, a head of science, suggested that there was room to experiment with group arrangements, particularly as more of his staff were now to be involved in working with trainees as class teachers or mentors.

Mentor D: I wanted the group of four trainees to have experience of a series of lessons with different staff, different age groups and different science subjects. I thought, why make my life difficult? They could do this. I gave them the timetables of the department and asked them to devise their own schedules. It took them a day, and they said it was a really worthwhile experience to understand the department and they learned more about each other's perspectives. They also observed lessons taken by an NQT and by a standard course student. I thought there might be tensions but all have enjoyed the experience.

Most trainee teachers enjoyed collaborative work, while a minority had reservations because of different teaching styles and different approaches to tasks.

Trainee A: We planned lessons as pairs, with advice from our mentor. We taught a starter or plenary part, and the mentor did the middle part. We discussed what worked at the end. Early on we worked together as different individuals with different ways of learning. Later, it was more a case of talking together more as teachers.

Trainee B: We had some good chats as a group; it felt less like a game of tennis, where ideas get batted from just one to another, and more like collecting a range of ideas. I think also, because we all have different ways of learning, we tended to make sense of lesson tasks in different ways and tackled the task of observing in different ways. I think because there were four of us and several mentors, it made us work together on arranged meetings as a group. It was a case of putting in different ideas rather than being critical friends.

Trainee C: We worked in a more specific way with an NQT who was part of the team of mentors . . . working on specific aspects of subject knowledge. We could relate to her more and we got an inside picture of starting work, looking for jobs. She was a bit nervous about our presence but she was using the interactive whiteboard in interesting ways.

A business department in another school has *become a very good host for special training days for trainees* as a result of the department's wholehearted commitment to mentoring. The department has been able to provide an induction day for twenty trainees from one university partner at an early stage of the training course. All staff members were observed by groups of two to three trainees during the day, and, at every opportunity, trainees and teachers were able to talk together about the experiences. Through their experience as mentors, the department staff were able to judge the language to use, the issues to highlight and the questions to set trainees to help them at a very vulnerable stage of their development. The visit was cited by all of the trainees as having a major impact in changing their perspectives about schooling and setting an ambitious agenda for the year.

The same subject department has worked collaboratively to provide a day's cross-curricular setting in which the group of trainees could explore *enterprise education*. The department provided resources, rooms and background support if required; the trainees planned creative tasks and managed the whole of a year group, with the intentions of providing both a good learning experience and showcasing the department for Key Stage Four Options.

With new work-force models appearing in schools, it is possible that the idea of department mentoring could be extended to include other adults as mentors. Some business enterprise schools have an enterprise manager to link together experiences across school departments and with partners outside school. Some larger departments have specialist teacher assistants assigned to them to work wholly within the department. Such colleagues have a wealth of experience, which could benefit trainee teachers, and would be available to part-mentor, if not on a weekly basis, then certainly at some stage during a placement.

Helping out is a two-way process

In the end, the strongest case for moving to department mentoring is likely to be based on what you get out of the experience as mentors, as well as the evidence of successful trainees moving on into new teaching posts. The old adage that a problem shared is a problem halved should be supplemented by the thought that a creative idea from a trainee that benefits one mentor should be shared for the benefit of the whole department, and the discussions that you will need to have as mentors will ultimately be discussions about your own practice and development.

Chapter 7

Mentoring and coaching

The helping relationship

Shaun Hughes

What are the similarities and differences between coaching and mentoring, and what can they offer to teachers? Mentoring is well established in schools as a support for trainee teachers, new teachers and those undertaking new roles and responsibilities. Additionally, coaching is increasingly popular as a strategy to support teachers' professional development and as a tool to help manage change. Both mentoring and coaching are gaining ground as ways of supporting people to improve performance and to meet the complex challenges that schools offer.

This chapter sets out to define and clarify these terms and to explore how those charged with supporting the learning of others – pupils, students or adults – can use a wide range of approaches that span the notions of mentoring and coaching. We hope to help the mentor/coach to understand her role more deeply and to improve her confidence in choosing and adapting effective and appropriate strategies.

It's worth saying a little about the development of mentoring and coaching. Traditionally implicit in *mentoring* are the support and nurturing offered by a mentor who has the knowledge, skills and attributes of the wise and trusted counsellor, someone who has travelled the trainee's path and understands the challenges. The mentor is there, as an expert, to advise, to guide and to use her greater understanding and skills to support the trainee. It has something of the apprenticeship model in it and has its roots back in the time of the guilds, before the industrial revolution.

Mentoring has a clear focus on performance. Leaders and managers will take trainees under their wings and initiate them into the ways of the organisation. Trainees are mentored in order to improve performance, however that may be defined. This can occur at every level within an organisation.

An important influence on the development of mentoring and coaching has been the sports world. Here, *coaching* has a very clear function with regard to raising achievement and performance. The argument has been deepened by a realisation that often the real barriers to progress may be not so much physical ones but problems of perception and confidence. This idea emerged from the sports coaching literature in the 1970s and 1980s and had an immediate impact in the business world, especially among leaders who, in some ways, saw themselves as similar to athletes.

This developing interest in mentoring and coaching in a number of different scenarios has led to a confusion of definition. The terms can mean quite different things in different settings. They can be used interchangeably, together as though they were synonymous and can even have reversible meanings. This ambiguity is in some ways healthy, in that it stimulates discussion and debate about what the roles of mentor and coach are, but it can be confusing, especially if one is working across professional boundaries. Often, when attending conferences or reading literature on mentoring and coaching, one has to begin by interpreting and understanding how the terms are being used.

Current writing and thinking in this area recognise this ambiguity of terminology and its potential for confusion. Recent research is beginning to work towards the idea of a 'helping relationship' within a 'developmental space', rather than being tied to the terms *mentoring* and *coaching* (Clutterbuck 2004).

The aim of this chapter is to contribute to this debate so that those supporting others in schools and colleges will gain clarity and confidence about the language used and a greater insight into the full range of strategies available. An underlying belief of this writer is that there is an important difference between mentoring and coaching, although the core skills of building rapport, listening for meaning and questioning for understanding are shared across the definitions. An understanding of this will provide the mentor with the ability to choose the appropriate strategy to support the trainee. A key belief is that, fundamentally, mentoring and coaching are about learning and understanding.

I shall use the term *mentor* as it is used generally in this book. This is someone usually involved in a professional relationship with an initial-teacher-training student or a new teacher, though it would also encompass mentoring (for example) new heads of departments or new head teachers. Implicit in this model is that the mentor has a greater knowledge than the trainee of the work involved and uses this to support, guide and advise the trainee. There may also be an assessment role to be undertaken. I shall use the term *coaching* where the coach is involved in a professional relationship with another colleague, supporting her learning and development, but does not necessarily need to be an expert in the colleague's field. In this relationship, the coach may support through non-directive strategies. It is not about providing answers or advice but more about enabling the trainee to understand and generate solutions. There is normally no formal assessment role.

The following two comments based on case studies clarify this distinction further:

> My *mentor* supported me brilliantly through my first year of teaching. She seemed to have an answer for every situation. She was kind but very direct. I found this difficult at first but as I got to know her I trusted her. She was fair and honest and her judgements of my teaching were always based on evidence, which helped me when I felt she was being critical. She did protect me in some ways and helped me build a relationship with the class. She was very experienced and helped me understand the standards.

> We started off informally really, watching each other's lessons when we could, and then discussing what we each thought. After the course on *coaching*, we realised we were peer coaches. It has helped us a lot; we now have a structure and the skills to support each other and I think we both agree that we have learned a lot about ourselves and our teaching. No one is in charge, we are not judging each other and it's just between us; but that doesn't mean to say that it isn't rigorous and challenging, because it is. I think we have both improved professionally as a result of coaching each other.

The National Framework of Mentoring and Coaching

This interpretation is in line with that of the UK National Framework of Mentoring and Coaching (DfES 2005). This framework was introduced in 2005 after wide consultation with teachers and was written specifically to help clarify the debate. It is very helpful and straightforward and is being increasingly adopted by schools.

The National Framework was developed by the Centre for the Use of Research and Evidence in Education (CUREE) as a guidance document to support those involved in mentoring and coaching. It suggests ten helpful principles that underpin effective mentoring and coaching. These are:

- a learning conversation;
- a thoughtful relationship;
- a learning agreement;
- combining support from fellow professional learners and specialists;
- growing self-direction;
- setting challenging and personal goals;
- understanding why different approaches work;
- acknowledging the benefits to mentors and coaches;
- experimenting and observing;
- using resources effectively.

It's worth considering these in the light of a *mentoring–coaching continuum* and the notion of a helping relationship.

The first of these core principles is the *learning conversation*. We discussed this with specific reference to mentor feedback in Chapter 4. This conversation, rooted in practice, seeks to articulate existing beliefs and practices in order to reflect upon them. It is part of the mentor's role to discover and understand the assumptions and beliefs that underpin the 'mental model' of the trainee, and to understand how she sees things. There are detailed suggestions about this aspect of the relationship in Chapter 5.

Inherent in all dealings within the helping relationship is the second core principle – a *thoughtful relationship*. This is about developing trust, requiring a sensitive awareness that learning of this kind is powerful and challenges preconceptions. The journey is emotional as well as intellectual. The effective mentor will work hard to build rapport and to think carefully about the relationship and how it is developing throughout the lifetime of the mentoring.

Professional mentoring and coaching relationships need to work within a *learning agreement*, often to an agreed and formalised programme. Everyone needs to know where they stand: there are explicit roles, and there is usually a clearly defined end to the relationship. There will be timetabled meetings and other protocols. Boundaries are agreed within these relationships, though they are not always clear-cut. There are times where the mentor and the trainee have a responsibility to recognise that the discussion is becoming a *counselling* discussion and inappropriate in this professional context. In reality, areas that touch upon self-esteem, self-confidence and emotional challenge do bring up issues that are relevant and may, in a few cases, require a reparative approach. Mentors, however, are not counsellors or therapists and, beyond acknowledging the importance of these personal issues, they may need to suggest that other professional help be sought. It is not uncommon for beliefs, values and attitudes, often developed from childhood, to be challenged in the early years of teaching as the trainee learns about herself. A helpful model here is to see mentoring and coaching as part of *a triangle of support*, comprising coaching, mentoring and counselling. Mentoring is 'putting in', coaching is 'drawing out' and counselling is (in this context) acknowledging.

The fourth principle, *combining support from fellow professional learners and specialists*, indicates that it is often a team of people who are involved in supporting new teachers. A key part of the mentor's role is knowledge of who should provide specialist help with practical systems or with professional issues. This sharing is important and mirrors the prevailing culture of the school and its view of supporting teachers.

In fact, the school's approach to the professional development of its staff has an important effect on the mentoring and coaching culture. In schools that have developed a positive culture, mentoring, coaching and peer coaching are well embedded and seen as part of the professional learning environment. Of course, schools are complex organisations, and many different views and positions are represented within the staff. At one school I know, trainee teachers or classroom assistants aren't allowed in the staffroom. Another caring and helpful role of the mentor is to be aware of their trainees' exposure to a range of viewpoints of other staff, some of which may be challenging!

Throughout the helping relationship there will be a *growing self-direction*. The trainee takes an increasing responsibility for her own professional development as skills, knowledge and self-awareness increase. This is a very pleasing and positive development. New teachers, towards the end of their first year, have a real desire

to feel they are fully competent professionals. The same is true of trainees, but care needs to be taken as to how much freedom to allow. It's a case of protecting trainees, while allowing them to make their own creative decisions and, possibly, mistakes. This highlights the importance of the mentor as expert and as a wise and trusted counsellor!

In terms of generating *challenging and personal goals*, target-setting is an important part of mentoring. It is discussed in some detail in Chapter 4. This should usually be a collaborative exercise. Targets, goals and objectives need to align, not only with the school and individual priorities, but also with the appropriate teaching standards. If the mentor is embracing coaching within his work, he is working across a *directive–non-directive continuum*. In dealing with prescribed competences, such as a set of teaching standards, he has to function at the directive end of that line towards appropriate, strategic target-setting.

Making the implicit explicit is a key responsibility and skill of the mentor, and we discussed this in Chapter 1. Through a learning conversation and 'questioning for meaning' (where the mentor leads the trainee through skilled questioning to a better under-standing), the reality of learning and teaching interactions can be explored. The mentor may know *why certain approaches work* and others don't, and this knowledge has often been built up over years of experience and reflection. It is very effective if, through skilful mentoring, the trainee can be supported in discovering this kind of learning for herself. This can be an exhilarating and empowering experience for the mentor as well, and supports the idea that mentors learn as much as trainees from mentoring relationships.

For example, to be able to support a new teacher attempting to reduce the most common low-level disruption experienced by teachers, talking out of turn (TOOT), the mentor needs to know what is going on and needs to be able to articulate this. It is sometimes not helpful to suggest to a new teacher that he watch an experienced teacher as an example of good practice. An experienced teacher will make behaviour management seem effortless and quite mysterious – 'I don't know how she managed to do this, if I tried some of the approaches I don't think they would take any notice of me!'. Of course, this expertise has been developed over many years. The teacher will have learned how to build successful relationships with classes and will know how to motivate and condition pupil behaviour. For many excellent practitioners, this has become second nature. It is developmental, however, if such observations lead to reflection upon ideas, suggestions and observations. The observation is only effective when discussed. Mentors and coaches gain enormously from this close analysis of their own and others' practice.

This is reflected in the next core principle – *acknowledging the benefits to the mentors and coaches*. Those operating as mentors in schools are often the most aware, skilled and articulate of teachers. There is a huge reservoir of experience, skills and reflective practice inherent in the mentoring role that sometimes goes unrecognised in schools. The benefits of mentoring to both mentors and trainees need to be celebrated and shared.

Training new teachers is not, of course, as straightforward as teaching a set of skills and behaviours. Much will be learned through observation and experience. A key mentoring role is to encourage this kind of learning and to create *an environment where new ideas and approaches can be tried*. One of the great benefits and joys of working with new teachers is that they are often full of ideas and enthusiasm and can stimulate new thinking. The mentor's responsibility is to be open to new ideas and to encourage the trainee to plan, and to evaluate with reference to direct evidence. Sometimes mentors need to let go of their usual ways of working. I had a trainee once who wanted to deliver an art lesson by asking the pupils to blow bubbles and then to observe, draw and paint them. Together, we discussed what could go wrong with this innovative idea with a fairly boisterous class. With certain protections in place, it turned out to be a very successful lesson that produced some excellent art-work as well as science understanding. As mentor, I had to balance my experience against the trainee's enthusiasm.

Using *resources* effectively is another core principle. Here, issues such as time management and the effective use of materials are appropriate focuses. The mentor may need to operate at the directive end of the continuum. It is quite appropriate to give clear directive guidance on the use of resources, based on experience. New teachers will find this immensely helpful.

The rest of the National Framework considers core concepts. The helping relationship is categorised as:

- *mentoring*: a structured, sustained process for supporting professional learners through significant career transitions;
- *specialist coaching*: a structured, sustained process for enabling the development of a specific aspect of a professional learner's practice;
- *collaborative coaching*: a structured, sustained process between two or more professional learners to enable them to embed new knowledge and skills from specialist sources in day-to-day practice.

Listening and sharing

The movement through specialist coaching to collaborative coaching is one of increasingly sharing learning experiences and mutual understanding. It has been used very successfully by mentors who are seeking to improve their mentoring practice or to explore their mentoring experiences. There are many similarities between the three core concepts, of which two are central to the helping relationship. They are *active listening* and *shared learning experiences*.

It's worth reflecting on these a little. Teachers are excellent at questioning, but often favour one particular kind, which aims to check understanding. Listening is a highly prized skill. To listen actively is difficult and requires practice. To some extent, being fully listened to is an unusual and quite challenging experience. Teachers have to learn how to listen effectively. For many years, a colleague and I would introduce listening skills as part of a mentor and coach training programme. We would ask the groups to under-take a role play where one person was the mentor, the other the

trainee. We provided the problem that would be the focus. We then observed the pairs as they engaged in the conversation. Often, the mentor would listen for a few minutes and then, unable to hold back, would start to dominate the conversation. We would observe this and feed this back. Of course, the mentors were not aware that this was the case – whereas the trainees always were.

Active listening takes practice and involves an awareness of, and control over, many different levels of listening. These can be categorised as *reflexive listening* – listening that is informed by the listener's own agenda, where what is heard is understood, sifted and responded to from the listener's point of view. This is, of course, a natural process, but one the mentor and coach need to be aware of. Another kind is *external listening* – listening to the kinds of language used and the way things are said as much as, or more than, listening to the content. In terms of building rapport, this can give the mentor valuable information as to the mentee's perspective. *Intuitive listening* concerns what the mentor or coach feels about the person he is working with. This is often about what is *not* said. It is paying attention to the 'music behind the words'. *Silent listening* is very powerful and very difficult. It is rare in our normal working lives to allow people the time and space to reflect in silence before speaking, to recognise a need for thought and then to develop it.

Listening, then, is a core and complex skill in any mentoring relationship. One might argue that it is the most important.

There is a complicating factor here, and that is that the mentor may also have an assessment role. This may be the case in teacher training or when new teachers are working towards national standards. There is no doubt that this will affect the kind of relationship that can be created. Simply knowing that, in the end, the mentor will be passing or failing or allowing entry into a profession is likely to add a layer of inhibition. This applies similarly to wider mentoring and coaching roles in schools. The performance management reviewer, for example, may have a role that recommends pay progression. These issues can be alleviated by skilled, collaborative and interactive mentoring. The more involvement the trainee has in the professional dialogue, the less of a problem this is likely to be.

We have talked in earlier chapters about dealing with problems and failures. One strategy that can help when things go wrong involves arranging for the trainee to have an *off-line coach*. This is someone who has no formal part in the assessment process but can coach the trainee in a safe environment. Another useful technique is to establish a team approach and to encourage positive feedback from other colleagues, and we discussed this in detail in Chapter 6. The National Framework suggests that, for specialist coaching, *buffer zones* should be created between coaching and other formal relationships, and that co-coaches should set aside existing relationships based on experience hierarchy, power or friendship.

The implications for mentoring teachers are complex and offer creative opportunities. Any competent mentor is likely to work across the mentoring–coaching (directive–non-directive) continuum. She will offer expert direction, but she is bound also to seek the trainee's development through self-discovery. A mentor seeking to improve her own mentoring practice should consider her position on this continuum and seek to extend and balance her repertoire across it, perhaps by using more non-directive interventions. But, structurally or personally, the full range of approaches may be unavailable to one individual. For example (as we've said), the mentor's assessment role may conflict with coaching-based, non-directive approaches. In some cases, a school may consider allocating to a trainee teacher both a mentor *and* a coach. In this relationship, the coach would be strictly and explicitly outside the assessment procedure. She may be closer in age or experience to the trainee than the mentor. She would question and support, but would not be in the position of expert director. She would work *collaboratively* with the trainee (see Chapter 3). Such an arrangement could be of enormous support to a mentee, as well as being developmental for the coach. A school may decide to run such a system, for example, for all trainee teachers, or it may initiate it ad hoc when a trainee is having difficulties.

The trainees, as professional learners, have a complex job to do here as well. This can be challenging, especially if they are struggling. The Framework suggests that they must respond positively to modelled experience and to questions and suggestions from the mentor, and take an increasingly pro-active role in their own learning, observing, analysing and reflecting upon their own and the mentor's practice. Fundamentally, they must think and act honestly regarding their developing skills and understanding. This requires very high levels of emotional intelligence, maturity and self-aware-ness (see Chapter 5). These are skills of reflection that can be supported and developed through sensitive mentoring.

The helping relationship

As an alternative way of understanding mentoring and coaching, this chapter proposes the notion of the 'helping relationship con-tinuum'. Teachers are often involved in professional helping rela-tionships. Some are formal and some informal. Informal mentoring has always been important and will continue to be so. It is a key element of school life: we all seek out the natural mentors.

Formal relationships, such as between mentor and trainee or induction tutor and new teacher, are increasingly important. The value of these relationships is increasingly being recognised as a key element in supporting professional learning – mentoring and coaching are now embedded in the teaching standards. Trainees and new teachers need help in many different ways. They need practical help with understanding the processes and systems of the school; they need help in developing their teaching skills, in planning, enacting and evaluating what makes an effective teacher. Trainee and new teachers need a particular kind of helping. Psychology can help here through providing some helpful models, practical guidance and a theoretical framework. The helping relationship continuum is a useful model to help us understand what particular stance we might take in supporting others.

Helping as a set of behaviours exists along various continua of approaches. We have already mentioned, for example, the *directive–non-directive* continuum. Being directive involves telling, the giving of instructions, whereas being non-directive involves supporting learners to come to an understanding of where they stand and to reach their own conclusions. You might like to consider where you would currently place yourself on this continuum in terms of your dealings with new and trainee teachers (Downey 2001):

Directive _____ Non-directive
(Push)   (Pull)

This question is powerful and reveals underlying beliefs about your understanding of the role of the mentor. Wherever you place yourself on this continuum indicates what sort of intervention you believe in. Other continua to ponder include:

Judgemental ——————————————— Non-judgemental

Diagnostic listening ———————————— Active listening

Effective helping seems to occur when the person being helped feels that the helper has understood the problem. She feels listened to and respected, and practical assistance is given to carry out the desired change.

Essential for this are two skill sets: *responsive* skills and *initiating* skills. *Responsive* skills are shown when the helper is able to demonstrate empathy, warmth, respect and *concreteness* – meaning the grounding of understanding in evidence and not vague generalisations. The helper is polite and pleasant and listens carefully, trying to see the problem from the point of view of the trainee and withholding judgement. This establishes a climate of trust and a supportive environment. This *responsiveness* is the base for the *initiating* activity that must follow. Having listened and understood, the coach or mentor must now ensure that things happen. This involves even more levels of empathy and genuineness, and perhaps some self-disclosure – yes, she too found it very difficult to keep some pupils quiet when they were talking! There needs to be an element of immediacy. This is a problem that needs resolving, as children's learning is involved. The helper's skills of responding in a positive manner, personalising the problem and supporting the learner in developing new strategies will lead to learning and so to exploring, understanding and acting – carrying out plans to achieve goals. The initiating skills are designed and used to help the learner become objective and, through this understanding, to establish a direction:

> I felt my mentor really helped me because she didn't rush to judge me – she listened and really tried to see things from my point of view. She did give some advice but she asked first if she could make some suggestions. I don't think I would have said no, but this simple thing helped me own the problem.

At the heart of this activity is the social learning theory model. Self-efficacy can be improved through performance accomplishment, vicarious experience and verbal persuasion.

Let's return to our problem of the new teacher not being able to achieve a reduction in TOOT. What would be an effective *helping* approach? I asked a number of experienced mentors how they might deal with this problem. The responses included:

- a very directive approach that used coercion as a strategy to ensure that pupils obeyed (if anyone talks when I ask them to be silent, they will be warned and if they continue, will be given a detention . . .);
- an approach that used observation of an experienced teacher;
- a close analysis of why the pupils were talking in the first place (Was the lesson boring? Was it at the appropriate level? Did the lesson engage the pupils?);

- a video to be made of the lesson to demonstrate to the trainee that her body language almost seemed to encourage a lack of attention;
- the mentor rehearsing what the trainee should say;
- a range of practical suggestions, such as identifying and moving the 'ring leader', adjusting the seating arrangements, using various sanction systems as advised by the school behaviour policy.

The variety of responses from mentors appropriately tended to cluster at the directive end of the helping relationship continuum. Here was a trainee who needed help from someone with more experience. This help needed to be sensitive and supportive, but also rigorous and challenging. Responses that were completely at the directive end, especially when accompanied by a judgemental approach and telling rather than listening and discussing, are likely to be less successful.

This kind of learning is not mechanistic, but is subtle and complex. Practical support can generate ideas around the suitability of the material, the scope of learning and even the kinds of language used. Observing how others do it can help. However, experienced teachers understand that this kind of teaching skill is often hidden. There may be issues that need a non-directive or coaching approach. Building rapport, listening for meaning and questioning for understanding – all used as foundations for a coaching approach – could do a lot to help the trainee to understand the situation. Withholding judgement can help explore issues such as a lack of assertiveness, a lack of awareness, a confusion as to what to do next and, crucially, an awareness of the emotional challenge, feelings and symptoms that are exhibited in these kinds of difficulty. This complexity of approach is perfectly in keeping with the nature of the problem. There tend to be no easy answers to these sorts of issue. The mentor can help provide the direction, but the map is not the territory. The right answers or ways forward with these dilemmas depend to a large extent on the person.

Responding to change

If we are then considering our work as mentors existing on this mentoring–coaching continuum, there are two further factors that can help our mentoring become more effective. The first is an understanding of the needs of the adult learner, and the second, an awareness of how people respond to change and challenge. Starting in teaching provides an immensely complex challenge with a range of different types of learning – learning how to be a professional, how to teach, how to be reflective and how to cope. The mentor's role can be seen very much as a supporter of this learning – the notion of the helping relationship continuum suggests that this is not the same as teaching. It is, rather, supporting the new teacher as she travels this very steep learning curve.

Everything that we know about adult learning suggests that a coaching, non-directive approach is the most effective. Elsewhere in this chapter, and throughout this book, we have helpfully compared the learning of new teachers with the learning of pupils in school. There are many useful parallels. However, we need also to accept that adults learn differently. Adult students are mature people and benefit better from an andragogical approach rather than a pedagogical one. They seek increasing self-reliance; their previous experiences are resources for self-learning and working with others; learning is most effective for them when it has a direct relevance to real and important situations and motivation is driven by internal incentives and curiosity, as well as by external rewards and qualifications.

An andragogical approach is one that establishes a climate of trust, collaboration and support. Planning is most effective when it is shared and collaborative. Central is the idea of mutuality – needs are identified together, objectives are jointly agreed – all activities, projects, contracts, methods and assessments ideally are shared and discussed. In these respects, the mentor takes on many characteristics of the coach.

One of the challenges for the mentor is to establish and maintain this kind of approach when working in a qualification context. Such a relationship is most effective, yet the pressure to direct can be overwhelming.

One view of mentoring has been seen as *facilitating*. Rather than managing and controlling learning, the facilitator provides the resources and opportunities for learning to take place. The *directive–facilitative* continuum runs in parallel with the *mentoring–coaching* continuum. The facilitator:

- focuses on the needs and objectives of the learner;
- focuses on the processes of sessions to maximise the effectiveness of contributions;

- is centred on others and seeks to build rapport;
- seeks to understand others' perceptions;
- is prepared to do a lot of listening;
- questions tenaciously, using open and probing questions to explore issues.

Considering these practices, we can see how close this is to the coaching state.

Trainee teachers are involved in a complex and challenging learning journey. They are not only learning the craft of teaching, but also continually reflecting upon their own behaviour and response to experience. This is true experiential learning – a continuous process grounded in experience. It is an action research cycle where the learner constantly relearns.

One of the most exciting and exhausting aspects of this process is the experience of change. This operates at many different levels, including that of fundamental personal change. Adult behaviour in a simple change model is based upon a combination of beliefs and assumptions. These are informed and driven by personal history, perceptions, psychological makeup and a whole range of other influences. Perhaps more than in any other profession, all of these facets of the personality are challenged.

Most new teachers, for example, need to come to a position with regard to behaviour management. As adults they will have had previous knowledge, skills and understanding in this area. They will certainly have attitudes. The reality of the role of the teacher will involve a recalibration of all of these positions. It is not just learning the tricks of the trade, but adapting to more underlying, quite fundamental perceptual shifts.

The mentor/coach has a delicate and vital role here. Understanding the cycle of learning and the implications for personal change is key to providing the right kind of support at the right time. An understanding that mentoring and coaching exist along a helping relationship continuum, and that this continuum runs beneath, through and within a cycle of learning and a learning experience that can be intense at times, is essential to a fuller understanding of the role.

This understanding that the mentor can operate as a coach and that mentoring is a dynamic, personalised process provides the mentor with a very powerful tool in supporting the learning of others.

The rapid adoption of coaching as a non-directive helping mechanism in schools to support people's performance and ability to cope with change offers a significant deepening of our understanding of how best to support trainee and new teachers. This new understanding has the potential to go far beyond a mentoring role, to enrich all of our professional relationships.

References

Clutterbuck, D. (2004) *Everyone needs a mentor: fostering talent at work*, London: CIPD.

DfES (2005) *National framework for mentoring and coaching*, London: DfES.

Downey, M. (2001) *Effective coaching*, London: Orion Business Books.

Chapter 8

Mentoring in a primary school

David Flint

Is the role of the mentor in a *primary* school different from that of a secondary mentor? There are many similarities. The things brilliant mentors have in common far outweigh any differences related to the phase of education. However, it is true that there are some aspects of the role in a primary school that are specific in their detail and application.

Working with parents

One such dimension is the relationship primary trainees will have with the parents of the children they teach. I remember a conversation with a trainee who was confident about her planning and preparation for lessons, even her use of formative assessment, but whose main concern was, 'How do I deal with the parents?'. Trainees in primary schools are likely to see much more of their children's parents than those in the later phases of teaching. This is particularly the case for those trainees working in the Foundation Stage, where they are likely to have *daily* contact with parents.

Experienced teachers and mentors rapidly acquire strategies for talking to parents and for involving them in partnerships to take their children's learning forward, but a young trainee, who may look only just out of school herself, may be overwhelmed by the challenge of talking to parents who are considerably older than her. This can lead to a tongue-tied, stilted conversation when parents deliver their children to the class in the morning, or at the end of the day – when bruises on heads have to be explained, or lost coats searched for.

We cannot expect trainees to be expert in this particular aspect of the teacher's role at the outset. I have experienced colleagues who still find dealing with parents challenging. Of course, this is a very important part of any training programme. The involvement of parents in schools has grown rapidly over the last ten years, and trainees will need help in deciding how best to harness this energy, which is powerful, but sometimes wayward. In some schools, parents form a central part of the education process and are involved in all aspects of the school – from working with teachers, teaching assistants and the governing body, to supporting school meals and dinner supervision. In other schools, it is still a major challenge to involve parents more closely in the education of their children.

Mentors must help trainees to understand the complex relationship between parents and teachers. But how? What is the best way? There is a danger here of the mentor separating theory and practice, as we outlined in Chapter 1. Of course, the mentor is able to model good *practice* in dealing with parents. This will help the trainee and give her confidence and strategies. But effective mentoring is more than this. Trainees need to watch, but not necessarily to copy, the work of mentors. They need help in understanding why some parents behave as they do. They need reassurance. They need to consider case studies of parental attitude and contact. The mentor must support these processes, which move beyond pragmatism.

Working with teaching assistants

A second important area of mentoring in primary schools in which mentors can provide invaluable support and guidance to trainees is in their relationship with teaching assistants. This is an area where, again, youthful looks and apparent immaturity can be a big disadvantage to a trainee (and, incidentally, to a teaching assistant). Now that it has become the norm to see at least one, and sometimes more, teaching assistants in a primary classroom, trainees often need some guidance on dealing with colleagues who may be more mature and who may have been teaching the class pretty much on their own for a long time. The knowledge that teaching assistants often have of the children, as well as of the school and class routines, is of course enormously useful, but it may be seen as a threat by youthful trainees. Mentors who have had experience of working with those teaching assistants are in a strong position to offer guidance and support, and perhaps to advise teaching assistants on the nature and sensitivity of these relationships.

One of the main areas in which trainees tell me they feel most intimidated is in *directing the work of* teaching assistants, especially

if the teaching assistant makes it clear that she does not approve of the direction or the director. This is an extreme example; in most cases, teaching assistants give invaluable advice to trainees and are very supportive. However, trainees will welcome suggestions on how to make the best use of the teaching assistants. They may need help to see that teaching assistants have talents that go beyond supporting less able children. This may, for example, involve asking them to work with the more successful groups of children, rather than with the less successful groups. Similarly, they need help to see the importance of sharing the planning before the lesson, to ensure that assistants know what is required of them. This can provide an ideal opportunity for assistants to share their experience and expertise with trainees – perhaps in pointing out any potential pitfalls, or identifying resources of which the trainee may not be aware. Teaching assistants should be seen as a major resource for both trainees and their hard-pressed mentors.

Staff structures and the cascade

Large secondary schools will have numbers of mentors working at different levels. The different sizes and structures of primary schools affect these mentoring relationships. Many primary schools have one lead mentor who, for example, is trained by the provider and has to cascade information to staff. This is a key part of the mentor role. For example, she will explain the nature of the monitoring and documentation that mentors have to complete for trainees – which change as the requirements develop and as new initiatives and strategies appear. When a primary school works with a range of different providers, mentors often find that the documentation is different for each one. This can make life very difficult for busy, hard-pressed staff, who have to explain this variety to equally busy class teachers.

The issue of mentors finding time and space to cascade fully to the rest of the staff still presents problems in some schools. In the best cases, time in staff meetings is set aside so that information can be passed on formally, rather than having to rely on brief conversations in corridors. The lead mentor is responsible for ensuring that all staff members are aware of when they will host trainees and of the nature of the expectations that the provider will have of the practice. Paperwork is a continuing issue with regard to hosting trainees, and mentors may offer valuable advice to training providers to help simplify and reduce it to a necessary minimum.

Subject range

Another way in which primary mentoring may present particular challenges concerns the range of subjects in the curriculum. Trainees need mentor support with this. Subjects may include not only the core subjects of maths, English and science, but also ICT, music, art, history, geography, design and technology, PE and RE. This is a formidable list for any teacher, but it does represent an important aspect of mentoring. Primary teachers are trained to deliver the full range of subjects, and some, especially those in smaller schools, have to do this. In some larger schools, teachers specialise, and mentors need to help their trainees to learn from these specialists.

Experienced mentors will be able to make sense of this with some confidence, but new mentors may well find this aspect of the role challenging. There are some areas to which they can turn for support in giving this advice. One is the website of the provider. Most websites will contain details of the courses being undertaken by their trainees. In many cases, partnership schools will have access to the provider's virtual learning environment (VLE) on which the full details of courses are displayed. This should help mentors to know exactly what the trainees have been studying before they arrive in the school. In this way, the mentors will be able to check on how much they can expect of their trainees in aspects such as teaching PE or delivering the literacy strategy.

The core of this issue is subject knowledge. In theory, there is such a vast amount of subject knowledge that no one individual could hold it in her head. In reality, teachers quickly learn what they need to know and when they need to know it. Trainees take longer to acquire this facility, which is pragmatic and essential, and helping them to do this is part of the mentor's role. By its very nature, subject knowledge is changing all the time, and, in recent years, the pace of this change in some curriculum areas has been frenetic. This, coupled with the drive to establish particular approaches to teaching core subjects through the respective strategies, has combined to make subject knowledge a major item for consideration by all providers and primary schools, as well as the subject of investigation by inspection bodies.

Although mentors are required to comment on subject knowledge in the lessons they see taught by trainees, it remains a concern that most comment sheets focus almost exclusively on aspects of behaviour management. While this is very important, and a key element in the development of any teacher, it is possible that, over several school experiences, a trainee may not receive any feedback on her performance in relation to the development of subject content. Trainees must be helped to work on all aspects of their subject knowledge and not simply those they find most enjoyable or easy to grasp. They need to audit and organise. Mentors should set agendas for feedback, and the development of this crucial factor should always appear. Of course, sometimes the mentor has reservations about her own subject knowledge, and she must be honest with both herself and her trainee and be prepared to work on plugging those gaps in the spectrum. No teacher can have at her command the full range of knowledge required in primary teaching. Admitting to your own deficits may be reassuring to the trainee, and may help him to build his self-confidence alongside his subject knowledge.

It is important to point out that subject knowledge *on its own* is not a major determinant of a trainee's ability to teach. But it is a relatively neglected area in relation to the training of many primary teachers. Perhaps it is felt, wrongly, that subject knowledge belongs properly to the secondary school. As teaching approaches develop, and new, integrated and cross-curricular approaches take hold, the importance of subject knowledge may actually increase rather than decrease, since it will be increasingly vital to track, for example, the inclusion of curriculum areas within cross-curricular planning.

Trainees with a strong subject knowledge are able to offer something special to a school, so that, for example, a trainee with an interest in music is able to give that curriculum area a boost. In this way, the whole school can benefit from taking trainees as part of their training programme. Similarly, in recent years, there has been a strong demand for trainees with specialisms in English or maths to help take forward the development of those areas within a school. Schools rightly look to providers to produce trainees who are up to date with the very latest developments in particular curriculum areas or particular approaches to teaching and learning. Schools must see that they can benefit directly from working with trainees.

The big picture

Up to now, we have examined some ways in which mentoring in a primary school has elements that may be particular to that phase of education. However, the key principles of mentoring are generic. As we have said in earlier chapters, mentoring is a partnership in training, based on a process of reflection and analysis that helps to drive progress. The challenges that primary trainees often mention and with which mentors can help include:

- lack of confidence
- behaviour management
- voice projection
- personality
- engaging with pupils.

These are areas with which primary trainees struggle, but they are also common to training and mentoring across the phases, and advice on them may be found in every chapter of this book.

The mentor can help trainees gain *confidence* through modelling good practice in the classroom – for example, in using technology such as the interactive whiteboard and, most especially, in understanding appropriate lesson structures such as learning objectives. The centrality of learning objectives is discussed in detail in Chapter 1. They apply equally in primary training as in other phases.

Supporting trainees in terms of *behaviour management* has been discussed elsewhere in this book. It remains one of the trainee's main initial concerns. Mentors can suggest useful behaviour management strategies that the trainee can employ, but, as we have said elsewhere, pragmatism isn't enough. The danger is that, faced with a challenging class, theory flies out of the window. The mentor must support the trainee, not just by demonstrating tactics, but by discussing with the trainee the relationship between theory and practice.

Mentors often find that trainees' understanding of some basic professional requirements is an area in which they can be particularly helpful. In this context, the use of the *voice* is a good example. In the primary classroom, the use of the voice may be paramount. Many trainees fall sick in their placements through sore throats and related complaints. They are not accustomed to using their voices as they need to in the classroom; there is a strong temptation to speak too loudly or even to shout when faced with a noisy class of thirty excited young children. Here, the mentor is able to offer advice related not just to which are the most effective throat sweets, but also to alternative strategies that will have the same effect. Some of the most effective teachers I have seen are those who speak very quietly to the children, in some cases so quietly that children have to strain to hear. This can be an effective approach, but one that may not work in quite the same way for the trainee. Exemplification, modelling and reflection are crucial – as we said in earlier chapters. The mentor's role is to help the trainee to understand *why* the children may be noisy at some times, and how this can be either avoided or managed, as well as to give advice on how best to speak to the children. Mentors need to help trainees to understand the nature and characteristics of acceptable noise levels and help them to understand the causes of noise and how it can be channelled to promote positive learning. For example, the arrival of a fire engine in the playground is bound to lead to excitement in the classroom and a raised level of noise. Mentors can help trainees to see how this excitement can be channelled into some rapid action, such as clearing the room and preparing to greet the firefighters when they arrive in the classroom. Raised levels of noise can lead to panic on the part of the trainee, who may feel that senior staff in the school will regard this as some sort of breakdown in behaviour management. There is a strong temptation to intervene very quickly to quell noise, and to shout in order to achieve this. Many learn quickly that this does not work, and, as brilliant mentors know, shouting often leads to more noise.

The issue of personality and engagement with the children can be one of the hardest elements in the teaching and learning scenario that a mentor has to deal with. I often receive calls from mentors saying, 'I just don't think she is cut out to be a teacher. She doesn't have the personality for it. She doesn't seem to want to engage with the children.' I am never sure exactly what this means. As teachers, we are a motley bunch; there are many different personalities in the profession. Such a complaint usually means that the trainee is too quiet, or lacking in confidence, or reluctant to address the class as a whole – or all of the above. An emphasis on collaborative working (as analysed in Chapters 3, 6 and 7, in particular) can yield very positive results. Without such approaches, the trainee who lacks confidence may resort to lessons in which the introduction is kept to a bare minimum, to be followed by tasks for all children, which may well be based on worksheets or practical activities. This is a reflection of a comment in Chapter 1 about the swing from planning teacher activity to planning pupil activity. The mentor needs to help the trainee to achieve a balance.

Some final thoughts for primary mentors

Do try to build a positive relationship with the university tutor. One way not to start this relationship is by saying, 'I've been teaching for twenty years, so tell me – have you ever taught?', or, 'When were you last in front of a group of five-year-olds?'. It may be an appropriate question to ask later in the relationship, but not at the outset. All tutors will have had some experience teaching in schools, which is likely to be extensive and successful. It's best to defer judgement until you hear what the tutor has to say about the trainee, and see how far it tallies with your own views. Do remember that training teachers is a job in itself and, while you may feel that you are an experienced teacher, the tutor probably has more experience of the training process.

Don't say (or imply) to the trainee, 'I've seen it all and done it all. Just follow my lead and you will be fine. What you do in college is OK, but this is the real deal where you find out if you can cut it.' This is the nitty-gritty/airy-fairy trap that we outlined in Chapter 1. The implication is that what the trainee has studied (possibly for three or four years) is of little or no value, and that practical experience is the only thing that counts. Of course, it is true that time spent in school is vital. It is also true that, in order for trainees to make sense of all the experiences they will have in a relatively short period of time, they need the inputs that most get in college. This linking of theory and practice is crucial to understanding teacher training. The mentor must stand at the centre of this continuum, not at one end.

Don't leave the classroom a few days into the placement saying, 'Right! I'm going to the staffroom to put my feet up: they're all yours!'. This may have been how your training proceeded, but we know better now. The 'deep-end' approach may feel bracing and realistic to the mentor, but it takes no account of the essential *training* function of the placement, which we discussed in Chapter 1. There will be a time to leave the trainee on his own with the class; this is a matter of professional judgement and will vary with the class and with the trainee. Some trainees will blossom when left to themselves, and their confidence will grow proportionately. Others may need a little longer before they are ready for this step. If in doubt, talk to the tutor, who should know the trainee and may be able to offer an opinion.

Do make time to meet the trainee for a scheduled weekly meeting at which you will be able to talk about last week's targets and set some for the coming week. Time in school is pressured, especially for busy mentors, but this is a key element of the trainee's progress, and the mentor is central to it. A quick conversation in the corridor is not a substitute for a good discussion of strengths, weaknesses and where to go next.

Do give positive feedback on lessons that you observe. In truth, it's easy to criticise any lesson. Negatives are easy to find; the trick is to be constructive in the points that you make. We discussed this in a number of earlier chapters, including Chapters 2, 4 and 5.

Do seek help if things start to go wrong. There will be a procedure to follow with a trainee who seems slow to improve. There are lots of people who can help. Talk to the provider and ask if this has happened with this trainee before. Ask the tutor to make an additional visit to talk to you and to see a lesson so that you can compare notes. Then, offer advice from both yourself and the tutor as to how the trainee can improve. A joint observation of a lesson is a very good way of ensuring that you are correct in your judgements of the trainee and that the tutor agrees with your comments. Sometimes, a mentor from another local school may be able to offer advice if you are stuck as to how best support a trainee. If you think that things are not going well and you can see that the children's learning is suffering, then take action and contact the provider and ask for support. The provider knows your importance to the whole training process and will respond to help both you and the trainee.

Do make sure you hold an initial briefing session with all the trainees in your school at the start of the experience. This will give you a chance to share basic but vital information about school routines and procedures, for example, for behaviour management, as well as other duties of a teacher, such as playground duty and school clubs and trips.

Do go to mentor training and briefing sessions with your provider. While you may feel that you have heard it all before, there will always be something new, and the more you engage with the provider, the more you and your pupils will get out of it. If you get the chance to take part in the steering committee of the provider, do take it, because this is a really good way to have your say in the shape and principles of the overall training. Many mentors have strong views about how the relationship between mentor, trainee and tutor should develop. Do not be afraid to express these. You are in an excellent position to be able to offer advice to the provider. This book is about your importance in the training process for new teachers, so do make the most of it.

Being a mentor in a primary school is one of the most rewarding jobs within the profession. It gives you the opportunity to build the next generation of teachers. Training, as we've said, is a *partnership*, because it involves the trainee, the children, the mentor and the provider. All parties in this partnership need to understand their role and be comfortable with it. Mentors, by virtue of the key position they hold in helping trainees to bring together the theory and practice of teaching, are central to the training process.

Brilliant mentors are rather like shooting stars – there for a short time and then gone – often because of promotion. This does mean that there is always a demand and an opportunity for new mentors to come forward, and it is vital to the health of the profession that staff members do continue to train as mentors and use their skills to help new trainees. It is an incredibly rewarding experience, especially when we learn something new from a trainee, or when someone who was very nervous and uncertain gains the confidence to blossom as a teacher and so grows as a person. It is a great privilege to be a mentor, especially in a primary school. Remember, too, that, in a relatively short period of time, last year's trainee may be next year's mentor.

Chapter 9

Mentoring the newly qualified teacher

Jacqueline Cuerden

Since 1925, when the United Kingdom Board of Education made its first attempts to forge links between the initial training of teachers and their first school appointments, there have been, unsurprisingly, a great number of changes and developments in induction policy and practice. In fact, the term 'induction' did not actually come into play until the early 1990s. Before that, a newly qualified teacher, taking up her first school post, would be known affectionately as a *probationer*, undertaking her *probationary year*, the main aim of which (apart from survival) was to demonstrate a satisfactory level of competence.

My own probationary year passed by with the usual frustrations and successes, which I have since learned are part of the job. The only real sense of being on probation was, I think, the afternoon when the deputy head announced that she was popping in to watch me teach Year 11. The lesson passed by without any major drama, and I really cannot remember what I taught that day, but the feedback I received afterwards remains with me some twenty years later. It consisted of two pieces of advice:

1   Don't let the room get too hot and stuffy.

2   Don't let the boys dominate my attention. (Did I realise that I was directing more questions to the boys than the girls in the class?)

I took note of the advice, and presumably I passed my probationary year. Nothing more was said, and there were no more observations.

Of course, this was not a satisfactory model, and when the probationary period was finally abolished in 1992, it was with a view to shifting the focus of the new teacher's experience from a period of assessment to one of professional development. The term *induction* was introduced, and this less threatening noun brought with it connotations of positive support, introductions and training.

Statutory induction, however, was not introduced in the UK until 1999, when the then DfEE set out a clear and structured framework for professional support and development for newly qualified teachers, together with a clear set of *induction standards* that had to be met if a teacher was to achieve *qualified teacher status* (QTS).

In 2007, the UK induction standards were replaced by what are now referred to as *Core Professional Standards*, part of the new *Professional Standards for Teachers* that have been introduced to assess the performance of all teachers at many stages of their careers.

The whole induction package has placed far more responsibility on schools and staff, who now formally supervise the professional development of new teachers and have the additional responsibility of completing regular, criteria-led assessments. Indeed, it is the school that determines whether the new teacher passes or fails her induction year. Perhaps you will be instrumental in making this life-affecting decision.

You may be, to use the common terminology, an *induction tutor*, by which we usually mean that you are in charge of the induction programme for your newly qualified teacher (NQT). You may be a head of department or faculty, and induction is yet one more burden added to your workload. You may be the official induction tutor for your school, in which case it will be your responsibility to oversee the induction of all NQTs in your workplace, although the actual mentoring and coaching may be undertaken by subject mentors. Perhaps you have been asked to support a new teacher because you are a member of a mentoring department.

We could argue that the term *tutor* is actually a misnomer. It suggests that you are going to have to teach your new teacher new skills – how to be a better teacher. This is not entirely the case. Your role is to support, mentor and coach your colleague through her first year of teaching and, most importantly, help to devise an *individualised* programme that will allow her to develop as a professional. Ways of creating and maintaining such approaches are discussed in every chapter of this book, but here I intend to offer some additional guidance with specific reference to qualified teachers. I hope, too, that teachers outside the UK will, while employing different job titles and working within different educational systems, find the following advice, hints and suggestions worthy of consideration.

The best possible induction

So, what can we do to ensure that our new teacher gets the best induction possible? First of all, it is a good idea to check out what the official entitlements are. Full details of this in the UK are available on the website of the Training and Development Agency (www.tda.gov.uk/induction), and most local authorities will also provide specific guidance to support the induction programme. Your new teacher will also have access to this information: induction is a two-way process. Encourage your NQT to familiarise herself with all the documentation and information. She has to take responsibility for her own professional development; you are there as an expert, experienced teacher to support her in this.

So, what are the entitlements?

In the UK, the NQT is entitled to:

- a *reduced timetable* (10 per cent fewer teaching units than is standard for a full-time main-scale teacher);
- an *individualised programme* of induction support, linked to objectives set in the Career Entry and Development Profile (CEDP);
- regular *meetings* with whoever is supervising the induction;
- a half-termly *meeting* to review progress;
- half-termly lesson *observations*, followed by verbal and written feedback;
- a meeting each term to discuss the *assessment*, which has to be carried out by the induction tutor.

This is only a broad outline, but you will see that it is a considerable, additional responsibility for you. Research shows that very few induction tutors are given additional time or financial reward for undertaking this task, which seems extraordinary given its importance.

I do know of teachers who have happily agreed to 'look after' the induction of a new teacher, believing it to be a sort of buddy system, which probably involves showing him the ropes, answering questions and offering a sympathetic ear when necessary. Of course, this is all very useful, but, as we have seen, the role demands a great deal more of your energy than that, and much of this activity will

inevitably happen in your 'free' time. So, before you agree to take on this role, whether in the UK or elsewhere, do make sure that you understand exactly what is being asked of you. You need to be explicitly clear on two key questions:

- What are the statutory entitlements for the new teacher?
- What support or time will you receive to allow you to carry out your professional obligations?

What's in it for you?

So, having looked at some of the background and thought about the demands of the induction tutor's role, why are you doing it? What's in it for you?

My own research, together with wider studies carried out by the General Teaching Council and other organisations, has shown that most teachers who have been actively involved in the induction process claim to have reaped considerable personal and professional benefits from it. Typical responses from induction tutors or mentors refer to improvements in their own teaching, enhanced professional knowledge and improved self-evaluation of lessons. Some teachers claim that it has 're-energised' them and 're-engaged' them with the profession. Generally, there is a feeling that, in supervising a new teacher, you are likely to become a more reflective practitioner yourself. Indeed, to do the job well, this is a necessity.

Personal attributes of a brilliant induction tutor

There is an interesting consensus among teachers surveyed about the personal attributes that an induction tutor should possess. A successful induction tutor should be:

- approachable
- experienced
- enthusiastic
- a good communicator
- supportive
- sympathetic.

A local authority professional, experienced in training NQTs and their tutors, comments, 'The best induction tutors are the ones who are really passionate about it and have the time to do it . . .'.

First impressions . . .

We are all familiar with the cliché that *first impressions count*, but it really is worth bearing in mind as you set out on your mentoring journey. Your NQT may appear very confident and professional when you meet her on that first day in September, but appearances can be deceptive. (Just think back to the trainee teacher you said goodbye to the previous term. This teacher may have been on the same training course. You know how nervous and apprehensive your student was feeling about his first teaching job. This new teacher will feel the same.) If you can, resist the temptation to join in the pre-staff-meeting gossip about holidays and the horrors of the alarm clock, and spend some time chatting to your NQT instead. Make sure that she can locate coffee, pigeonholes and toilets, and introduce her to a couple of members of her subject department (preferably, the friendly, sociable, non-cynical ones who will be happy to guide a new teacher through the first day, which often consists of a confusing and frantic dash from one meeting to another). This is especially useful if your own role takes you off for a good part of the day to other managerial duties.

Try to find some time at the end of that first day for an informal chat with your new teacher. This will allow her to ask all the questions that she has thought of during the day. Try to give your undivided attention at this point: she needs to feel that you are going to be approachable and willing to support her. Take some time to look at her timetable with her, discuss resources and make sure that she has all the information that she needs to help her function effectively and efficiently in that crucial first week of the new term. Ensure that she understands the school's behaviour policies and how the sanctions and rewards systems operate. (Ideally, your new teacher will have already been given all this information, but it's always worth checking.)

Pencil in your diaries the date of your first 'formal meeting', preferably within the first fortnight, but make sure that she knows that you will be around to help her. Encourage her to consult TDA and (if appropriate) local authority or school materials on induction in readiness for your first formal meeting.

The first formal meeting

You will have many informal corridor and staffroom conversations, but these do not replace the essential programme of formal meetings. These meetings need agendas and recorded outcomes, and they need a settled and private location. The main item on the agenda for the first such meeting should focus on the NQT's perception of her development needs, and this may well be presented as a written profile completed in the final stages of training. In the UK, this is known as the *Career Entry and Development Profile* (CEDP), and the new teacher should be asked to bring it along to the meeting. Leave plenty of time for her to raise issues and ask questions, but remember that the purpose of this meeting is to try to work out what your new teacher considers to be her strengths and weaknesses, and to ascertain whether the objectives she set for herself at the end of her initial teacher training are still relevant and applicable with regard to her new post and its particular demands.

Setting SMART targets

The new teacher will be used to setting herself targets and objectives: she has been doing this throughout her initial teacher-training programme. Indeed, many of the induction activities will be more familiar to her than they are to you. At this stage, she needs to be aware from the outset that the targets she sets herself have to be consistent with the core professional standards set by the government, as well as appropriate to the context in which she is working.

The SMART acronym is particularly useful here and will make your meetings with the new teacher focused and productive. SMART targets, as we outlined in Chapter 4, are specific, measurable, achievable, realistic and time indicated.

Your NQT arrives at a review meeting flustered and angry because her lesson with Year 9 has just been, in her words, a total disaster. She is keen to discuss individual pupils and feels upset that the lessons she has worked so hard to prepare are being undermined by a handful of students. You are aware that time is slipping away and this meeting is in danger of turning into a lengthy chat about the horrors of adolescence. She tells you that she wants to make the management of this class one of her 'targets' for next time.

This is the moment you've been waiting for! You ask her to be specific in formulating a target here. What is it that she can specifically attempt which might improve the general standards of behaviour and learning in that class?

As she analyses the situation more closely, it becomes apparent that the most disruptive pupils are all of low ability. They are sitting together, and they seem to start the disruptions within the first ten minutes of the lesson. Further discussion establishes that your NQT is not planning for differentiation within the lesson, believing that students in this class will all be working at a similar level, and that differentiation may be left to outcome.

As you encourage her to explore this further, she starts to realise that, if she produced differentiated activities for the weakest students, allowing them to access the lesson from the outset, then the level of disruption may be reduced. She now sets a *specific* target: *to produce differentiated learning materials, which will allow all students to access the lesson.* This target is also *measurable*. If the new, differentiated lesson plans are successful, this will be reflected in the improved performance of the weakest students being targeted. This target is *achievable*, especially if you discuss with her how she is to manage it, so that differentiated plans can be designed and implemented in the classroom. It is relevant and *realistic*, and a deadline *time* may be set for this change in planning protocol to take place. A generalised target has been revised into a helpfully specific one.

Lesson observations and feedback

In the UK, the statutory guidelines stipulate that the new teacher must have his teaching observed within the first four weeks of induction. The observer – usually the induction tutor – must hold QTS and be relatively experienced. It is worth spending some time planning for the observation and discussing the lesson with the new teacher before the 'big day' dawns.

Although your new teacher will be used to being observed, coming as he does from a teacher-training course, he will no doubt be rather apprehensive about this first observation in school. He will be keen to make a good impression, and may feel a little unsure about what you will be looking for.

You need to reassure him by explaining the context, purpose and focus of the forthcoming observation. You will perhaps say,

> I will be coming in to watch you teach your Year 10 class on Monday. Don't feel that you have to put on a special performance for me. I will just want to see a well-structured, objective-led lesson. I want to get an idea of how you manage the students and to what extent your learning objectives are being met. I would be grateful if you could let me have a copy of your lesson plan on the day. Here is a copy of the lesson observation pro forma I am expected to use. It might help you to know what I have to fill in about you! In future, of course, we will agree a specific focus in advance of each lesson. I have noticed that we are both free after lunch on Monday; perhaps we can meet in my office at 1.40 p.m. so that I can give you feedback?

A semi-formal (but friendly) statement like this is necessary to reassure the NQT. The intended observation may well be general, but the new teacher will be thankful that he has some idea of what you are coming to look at. By asking him for a copy of his lesson plan, you are suggesting a degree of formality, and your new teacher will know exactly what is expected of him. The copy of your lesson observation pro forma will empower him as he plans and organises his lesson. Finally, the arrangements for the feedback meeting send out the message that you are taking the observation seriously, as part of your role, and that you are keen to devote quality time to developmental discussion.

In the UK, induction tutors are expected to observe at least six lessons in the year, and each one should be followed by verbal and written feedback. After the first general observation, you may suggest one or more specific areas that your new teacher may wish to focus on in the weeks or months ahead. Subsequent observations will allow you to monitor the new teacher's progress in those areas.

Written feedback

There is appropriate advice on written and oral feedback throughout this book; you may want to look particularly at Chapters 4 and 5. Of course, you should aim for consistency and link your observations to the NQT's focus for the lesson and, most importantly, to the core standard against which the new teacher will ultimately be judged. Do try to look for positives in the lesson. Where there are areas for improvement, try to offer a suggestion for a strategy or approach. Consider what further support the new teacher may require to enable her to meet the standards. What SMART targets need to be set and worked towards?

The post-observation discussion

Research has shown that new teachers find that lesson observations and the subsequent discussions with their induction tutors are vitally important to their progress and development during the induction year – providing that they are genuine discussions.

The meeting should be held somewhere comfortable and private, away from the threat of interruptions. The arrangement of the chairs is quite significant. If you place the chairs directly facing each other, the meeting may feel threatening or overly formal. Try having the seats at right angles to each other.

Any feedback discussion should begin with the mentor asking the new teacher for her own evaluation – especially of the strengths of the lesson. The three key questions ('What were they meant to learn? Did they learn it? How do you know?') should figure early and prominently in the feedback. It may be useful to ask the new teacher to reflect on low-, middle- and high-achieving pupils. What did each child learn? How did the teacher adapt to ensure that all pupils derived the maximum benefit from that lesson? Could anything have been done differently? Were there any surprises?

There are lots of questions here, and there is a good reason for this. In thinking and reflecting on the lesson in this way, the new teacher will actually be learning and developing her skills as a reflective practitioner. She will learn more this way than by simply listening to your commentary on the lesson and your suggestions and advice. Of course, there is a time and place for you to give your thoughts, but if you find that, at the end of the meeting, you have done all the talking, then perhaps you need to consider how the balance can be redressed the next time. In fact, this is a common weakness in mentor and tutor feedback. The expert has much to say, but the NQT must do most of the talking if she is to further develop her reflective and evaluative practice.

Coaching and mentoring the new teacher

A brilliant induction tutor will be keen to employ a range of coaching and mentoring techniques to help the new teacher develop professionally. Much has already been said in this book about the coaching and mentoring of trainee teachers, especially in Chapter 7, and the same techniques can be used with newly qualified teachers (and indeed with any colleagues!).

Personally, I have found the GROW coaching method to be most appealing. Perhaps it's the mental image that it evokes . . . a new teacher springing up like a tomato plant from a compost bag.

- G is for the *goal*. What would you (the NQT in this case) like to achieve?
- R is for current *reality*. Where are we now? What is the situation at present?
- O is for *options*. What are they?

- W is for *winning commitment*. How much do you want to achieve this goal?

In this approach, the focus is on the new teacher thinking about the areas that need to be developed and how to achieve this. This links well with the SMART targets mentioned earlier in the chapter. It's also particularly helpful as we start to consider establishing an individualised programme of support for the new teacher, an essential and statutory element of the induction year.

Planning an individualised programme of support

The good induction tutor will ensure that the new teacher has access to significant members of staff, INSET, new teachers' meetings and so forth. The *brilliant* induction tutor will ensure that she has worked with the new teacher to draw up an action plan that will provide personalised support and professional development for the NQT.

This is, in fact, a statutory requirement of induction in the UK, but, sadly, it seems to be an area that is often overlooked. Many schools run courses in the first term that are designed to introduce all new members of staff to the policies and practices of the school. Of course, these courses are useful and helpful, especially in the early days. The problem is, however, that one size really does not fit all, and, as useful as this generalised INSET may be, it may still not address crucial, individual areas that the new teacher may need to develop.

Way back at that first formal meeting, when the first lesson observation has taken place, and the first SMART targets are being set, the brilliant induction tutor and the new teacher really need to plan a programme of experiences and activities that will enable the new teacher to meet the core standards. This individualised programme is something that can be addressed in the additional 10 per cent non-contact time that, as we've seen, is allocated to every new teacher in the UK.

How to make effective use of that additional non-contact time

Each new teacher will need to develop certain areas of his teaching, planning, marking, behaviour management, assessment strategies and so on if he is to meet the core standards by the end of the induction year. As a new professional, he must take responsibility for this, with your support. He should be encouraged to devise a programme, with your assistance, and follow his plan conscientiously, thereby making the reduction in his timetable productive and worthwhile.

You have a free lesson – a precious hour to work on the many commitments you have in school. Of course, you need a coffee first, with a post-Year 9 chocolate biscuit, and then you'll begin. Perhaps, though, your emails need checking first. A knock on the door, and a miserable-looking boy tells you he has been sent from Mr Jones: he has been misbehaving. Suddenly the bell rings, and the free lesson is over. Nothing has been achieved. Our new teachers can be distracted and procrastinate in exactly the same way. The point is that the additional time is intended to be devoted to meaningful and productive professional development activities. Let's face it – they won't get that sort of opportunity again!

So, as a brilliant induction tutor, what sort of recommendations can you make to your new teachers about the best ways to spend induction release time? Obviously, the suggestions you make will depend on your new teacher's strengths and weaknesses. The following are some ideas the new teacher may consider. It is not, of course, an exhaustive list, but activities such as these should focus the new teacher's mind on what should be happening:

- lesson observations of experienced (and less experienced!) teachers;
- speaking to the school's Additional Needs Coordinator;
- discussion with the school's Gifted and Talented Coordinator, asking for advice in planning to meet the needs of the most able students;
- observations of experienced teacher teaching EAL students, with a post-lesson discussion about the strategies employed;
- meetings with members of the school's senior management team to discuss school policies;
- attending school council meetings to find out more about *pupil voice* initiatives;
- moderating coursework alongside an experienced departmental colleague;
- planning a medium-term scheme of work with a more experienced colleague;

- writing pupil reports alongside a more experienced colleague and reading previous reports in order to become more familiar with the in-house reporting style.

The new teacher, in planning her programme of activities, should ask herself what she needs to do to become a more effective teacher, and whether the activity she has chosen will enable her to achieve this outcome. Activities must be clearly linked to the specific objectives she has agreed with you and the SMART targets she has set for herself.

Research has shown that the activities that the new teachers find most useful are linked to lesson observations, and yet this is an induction activity that is frequently overlooked or neglected. As well as running a series of progressive and targeted observations, a mentor needs to structure the dynamic reflection (discussion, reading, comparison and synthesis) that follows them.

In summarising these activities, it's worth considering what might be familiar or reasonable to a new teacher and what might still be novel and challenging. In this connection, it's a good idea to consider how the mentoring of an NQT might differ from that of a trainee teacher. It's common for a mentor of trainee teachers to become an NQT mentor, and it's unsurprising that she may see the new job as a natural extension of the old one. Certainly, as we've said repeatedly, they are not dissimilar; much of the advice throughout this book applies to both. Some of the associated procedures – reflection, evidence-building, standards compliance – look remarkably the same. However, in terms of content and ability, we might expect some differences. We should expect to discuss issues with our NQTs that might well be considered advanced and even unrealistic during the earlier training. With our NQTs, we should be able to analyse issues such as differentiation, inclusion and assessment for learning as they present themselves. We should be considering how learning theories (such as constructivism) might be put into practice. The pragmatics of survival may well have dominated the initial training, but now, as we work with and develop our young professionals, this must no longer be the case.

Staying aware of the new teacher's feelings

Teaching is, as we know, an exhausting, emotionally charged, frustrating and demanding profession. You are an expert teacher,

yet you will probably experience the emotional highs and lows of the job on a weekly (if not daily!) basis. Imagine, therefore, how your new teacher must be feeling as she struggles to cope with all the demands of the job and the pressures of induction. Appearances can be deceptive. A talented, confident NQT may seem to thrive, and relish every moment. The induction tutor needs to ensure that this is actually the case. Do keep a discreet eye on your new teacher. Take time to sit and chat, or call into her room at the end of the day. Look out for signs that she may be over-committing to school activities, taking on too much or drowning under a sea of paperwork. Have a quiet word with trusted department colleagues and ask their opinions on how your new teacher is feeling. She may feel uneasy about admitting her problems to you, especially as she knows that you are the person who will be completing her termly assessment reports.

Be particularly aware of her emotional and physical health around the end of the autumn term. In the UK, this is a cold and dismal time of year. The staffroom and classrooms are full of people coughing and sneezing and sharing their germs generously in the dry, centrally heated environment. For the new teacher, the novelty of the new job, new classroom and new pupils is wearing thin, diminishing under the relentless pressure of marking, planning, parents' evenings and progress reports. Her voice is feeling the strain, and she seems to be succumbing to one virus after another. The Christmas holiday seems an age away, and the first induction assessment is looming.

The brilliant induction tutor takes all this into account and tries to help the NQT through it. Sometimes, a small gesture is all that's needed. Try offering a lesson plan that has worked well for you and that may be designed to reduce the marking burden at a busy time. Take a cup of coffee into your new teacher's classroom at the end of the day and ask how things are going. Just making yourself available for an informal chat from time to time will be much appreciated by the NQT, who may well have questions and doubts that perhaps seem too trivial for a formal meeting, but can create worries and anxieties if not addressed. Look for something that your new teacher has done that is worthy of praise, and make the time to go and praise her and to thank her for her efforts.

The assessments – completing forms and gathering evidence

Ultimately, the responsibility for providing evidence to support the new teacher's progress against the core standards rests with the new teacher himself. He will have been using his additional non-contact time to improve and develop his professional expertise and should have kept documentary evidence wherever possible to support his claims in this area. The formal assessments, however, rest with the induction tutor. The main thing to consider here is that, if you have followed the guidance set out by the government and ensured that the new teacher has been granted all his statutory entitlements, then there really should be no unpleasant surprises for anyone when the assessment forms are due for completion.

The assessment meetings

The three formal assessment meetings are extremely important for the new teacher, and, however busy, tired or stressed you may be feeling at the end of a term, it is vital that you put these meetings in your diary and allow plenty of quality time to review your new teacher's progress with her and discuss the assessment documentation. Encourage your NQT to prepare for the meeting, especially if concerns have been expressed about any aspect of her performance. Try to find a time within the school day, if at all possible, to hold the meeting, and ensure that the venue for the meeting is private, comfortable and non-threatening. Some induction tutors go to the NQT's classroom, a place where she will feel at 'home'.

As a brilliant induction tutor, you will have assisted and supported your NQT in devising her individualised programme of support. You will have met with her regularly and discussed her progression against her SMART targets and her developmental objectives linked to the core standards. You will have observed her lessons at least six times during the year, and you will have given her positive, prompt and constructive feedback in writing and in the post-observation discussion. As the intuitive, sensitive and empathetic individual that you are, you will have discreetly monitored your new teacher's emotional equilibrium during the year and done your best to offer some 'tea and sympathy' during the low points. You will have helped your new teacher to become a fully fledged member of the profession, ready to take on the responsibilities and challenges of her second year of teaching.

But – what if the new teacher is failing?

Sometimes, for any number of reasons, the new teacher may struggle to meet the core standards, and, even though you have put in all the strategies listed above, you may still not see the standard of performance that you would expect. What then?

The most important thing to remember when faced with a failing new teacher is to seek advice from the school's induction coordinator, an experienced senior teacher or head teacher, or the local authority representative who has responsibility for NQTs. Do not bury your head in the metaphorical sand and hope that things will get better. Do not be tempted to avoid the problem in order not to damage the NQT's confidence. The situation may well improve, but it is in everyone's interest if the new teacher is alerted to your concerns and that steps are taken to put in an extra layer of support for her well before the final assessment. You must also ensure that you keep detailed and accurate records of all your meetings and conversations with your new teacher. Document all the strategies that you have helped her to put in place, and link everything to the core standards as you maintain these records.

It is rare for a new teacher to fail induction, but it can and does occasionally happen. If it really seems to be the case that the new teacher, even with additional support, cannot meet the core standards, then it is usually the best solution for the local authority representative to ask the new teacher to leave before her third term. The NQT will then, in the UK, have the opportunity, should she wish to do so, to restart and complete her third induction term in another school at another time. The fresh start that this situation affords may well result in a successful outcome. We must remember that, if the new teacher had remained in the school and failed the final assessment, then she would not have been eligible to teach in a maintained, or a non-maintained special, school again.

Goodbye induction . . . hello performance management!

As the year draws to what is, for the vast majority of new teachers, a successful conclusion to the induction progress, it is time to encourage your NQT to start thinking about his professional targets and objectives for his second year of teaching. In the UK, this will involve the completion of what is known as *Transition Point Three* of the CEDP, and this process is designed to dovetail very neatly into the performance management cycle, a statutory requirement for all teachers.

A good induction tutor will remind the new teacher that this needs to be done before the end of the summer term. The brilliant induction tutor, however, will find the time to discuss the new teacher's professional aspirations with her and help her to choose targets that will be meaningful and constructive in allowing her to achieve her goals and to continue to progress into and through the next stage of her career.

Chapter 10

Dear Mentor . . .

Trevor Wright

We have examined many mentoring practices and attitudes and heard a range of voices. The trainees have not been absent from any of the chapters of this book, but perhaps it's finally time to hear directly from them. Here are some of their experiences, drawn from them at various stages and in no particular order. Whether telling positive stories or making polite suggestions, these reflections share a surprising but typical intensity.

When a PGCE student first begins their teaching practice they might have an idea of what they *want* or hope to get from a mentor but until they start their placement they don't really know what it is they *need*.

In my case, I wanted someone who would be approachable, friendly and knowledgeable, someone who would become a friend. It wasn't until I began my placement that I realised that what I *needed* was someone who was willing to give me confidence and to be supportive when I hit any bumps in the road.

What I got was exactly that.

I was very lucky in my first placement and I was delighted that my mentor supported me throughout. For example, when I had a period of less positive teaching experiences with my sixth-form group, my mentor quickly stepped in to support and guide me. She discussed the issues with me and spoke with the class teacher on my behalf. She then sat and went through my lesson plans with me and she was able to help me realise that it wasn't my teaching or planning that was the problem, it was my confidence in a sixth-form classroom in front of an 'old-school', experienced teacher. Having had this support, I identified the cause of my problems and I was able to reflect and treat the symptoms.

We became good friends, and she helped me to feel confident in the classroom and in my own abilities. I was also made to feel like I was a part of the department (being invited to all department meetings and even the Christmas night out) and I was encouraged to go to any member of staff for help or reassurance. This foundation was essential to the continued success of my training, and I think it is important that mentors realise they need to give trainee teachers a good grounding in their first placement, so that they can begin their later placements confidently and successfully.

When I began my next placement, I hoped for the same kind of mentor again, someone experienced, enthusiastic and supportive. I also hoped for the same kind of experience again. In the first few weeks of my placement I realised that this would be an entirely different experience.

My mentor was a male head of department. My previous mentor had been a female classroom teacher with no other responsibilities. Straightaway I discovered that, although he was very experienced, pleasant and friendly, he didn't always have the time. It was sink or swim.

I needed to be profoundly organised; able to get on completely by myself; direct my questions to anyone with a pulse when I needed answers; get involved and use my initiative in order to reflect and adapt. At first I thought that this was hell. It was the complete opposite of what I had been given in my comfortable first placement and it was frightening and intimidating. I was starting all over again, back at the beginning. My mentor and I didn't always agree, and, at times, I found myself challenging him or being challenged myself. It was the first and only time I had second thoughts about being a teacher.

As weeks and terms passed by I realised that although this wasn't what I had hoped for, it was what I had *needed*. My mentor's approach had meant that I was quickly developing into a confident, strong classroom teacher and that I was learning to rely on myself instead of others. I was taking full responsibility for my training and

I was succeeding; this gave me constant gratification. I was still enjoying teaching, and my observations were continually positive. My relationship with my mentor became constructive, and when I had a bump in the road he was supportive; when I was struggling to engage a particular pupil he gave me advice, and when I needed to speak to him *he found the time*. When I was frustrated with a lack of communication with some other members of the department, my mentor found the time to sit down with me after school. Together, we were able to decide on a plan of action that would be professional but would see me solving the problem myself. The reassurance from him (that I had done the right thing in taking my problem to him) was vital in making me feel comfortable and supported in my training. That two-way, constructive relationship is important for the trainee and is fundamental in being a brilliant mentor.

I can't say that this second approach is the right one; it certainly wouldn't be right for someone who was lacking in confidence or having problems in the classroom. It definitely wouldn't be a suitable approach for someone who was poorly motivated or extremely disorganised. Nevertheless, it was right for me at this time.

A good mentor is one who can support the trainee teacher in becoming confident in their own teaching ability and can find the time, now and then, to have a supportive chat.

A constructive, two-way relationship is vital and will ensure the trainee keeps the mentor up to speed with their development and any worries.

Most importantly, a brilliant mentor can see what the trainee teacher *needs* at different times of the course and will support them accordingly.

'I'm just putting the boys to bed – can I phone back in ten minutes?' My first mentor gave us her home phone number on our first day. I'd hoped for a mentor who was dedicated, enthusiastic and inspirational and I certainly got that. She threw us in at the deep end – we taught every single lesson from day one – but supported us throughout the entire process. She developed our reflective skills through asking the right questions: 'What questions will you ask next time?'; 'Why do you think Mark said that?'; 'How do you think Jenny feels about this topic?'. Our mentor meetings generated very specific targets, such as 'focus on transitions', 'develop direct questions', etc. Taking a day out of half term to explore schemes of work, help us rationalise objectives and guide us towards relevant and suitable outcomes reflected her commitment. We were included in training workshops on group work, boys in literacy and working with teaching assistants. In fact, we were treated like NQTs who had development programmes to work on, and this professional attitude towards us inspired a professionalism and self-respect in terms of organisation, presentation and reflection.

However, although my next mentor also treated me as an NQT, it was in a more detrimental way. I moved from my first school with support, positive reflection and mutual respect to an environment where the expectations of me were extremely high, the department was cold, and my experience was belittled. They had difficulties realising that I was still in the embryonic stages of my training and placed a lot of pressure upon me in terms of the amount of texts I had to teach, the expectations of my lessons and the fact that every minute aspect of my early lessons was torn apart in a negative way. Many staff did not know how to complete an observation form properly, and most criticised elements of teaching, especially at the beginning. Criticisms included 'use more direct questions', even though I knew no names and had no seating plans, an example of the high level they expected of me. I found the mentor and department to be very inflexible and had to ask permission to adapt my timetable. I was reprimanded for personalising the lessons that existed on the system, as I was expected to teach them rigidly, an incident that reflected the attitude of my mentor and the department in general.

After a month into my PGCE course I was assigned to my first placement. I expected this to be an introduction to the practicalities of teaching coupled with a first experience of working in a classroom. I arrived at the first placement with high hopes that my

mentor would support me in my attempts to bring the theory I had been examining over the last month at university into the school context. This, I had imagined, would mean looking at schemes of work and lesson plans and adapting these for my own classes.
I hoped to be involved in planning myself and was looking forward to having the advice of an experienced teacher to support my trials. However, the experience I had did not match those hopes. This was in part because my attempts to discuss schemes of work and lesson plans were met with a dismissive look, and I was made to feel quite ridiculous for even asking if I may look at existing examples of these in the school. Apparently they did not exist, and I should have been aware of that. Overall, I was given the impression that there were inconsistencies between the university's expectations of the placement and those of the school. Attempts to bring these discrepancies to the school's attention via the professional mentor did not have any effect.

By comparison, the experience I had at my second placement school was quite different. Schemes of work based on the National Curriculum were readily available. Where my observations or requests were unrealistic or naïve, this was pointed out in a supportive and constructive manner. At no time was I made to feel that the school was contradicting the teaching I had been receiving from the university – whereas quite the opposite was true in my first placement.

When I finally began training, I had ideas and thoughts on what my experiences would be like. When told of my first placement I was anxious to meet my mentors. My first meeting with my first professional mentor was to set the tone for all other meetings.
He spoke to all of us and there was a sense that when you spoke he was actually listening. The most important thing I remember was when he said 'give new things a try'. Use this time to try new ideas and 'steal' ideas from other teachers and subjects to enhance your teaching. He was one of the busiest people I have ever met. However, if I was sitting on my own in the department, he would always ask how I was doing. I always felt I was working *with* him and

sometimes I would ask him for advice in areas. He was always honest about his limitations and sports where he was unsure, and I felt that if he had areas in PE where he was weak then I didn't have to be embarrassed about not knowing a lot about certain sports. This was someone who I looked up to yet never felt I was looked down upon. He was always willing to offer advice, yet not make me feel ignorant for not knowing. More often than not I knew when I had made mistakes and didn't need someone to keep reminding me. Luckily, both mentors seemed to acknowledge this. A major positive was the feeling that they too made mistakes and would often spend time in the department discussing their own lessons and asking each other how to improve.

A major aid in my relationship with both these mentors was their willingness to get to know me as an individual. I never felt like a student in this department but a colleague who was learning alongside the other teachers.

To this day I do not know anything about my professional mentor. I was told she would be very busy. I did not have meetings with her and made contact via a pigeonhole and the Internet! I come from a place where talking to another person face to face is still seen as the most effective way of communication. I found my professional mentor to be almost non-existent and therefore when I was having difficulties she really didn't cross my mind as a person I could talk to. On top of this I had been told she was an exceptional teacher and incredibly organised. Straightaway I felt inferior and may not have wanted to be reminded of everything I felt I wasn't at this low point of my training.

I feel when we do speak I am being spoken down to. Almost every observation has ended in a negative, and there were conversations and comments that have dented my confidence so much that I often sat on my own in quietness, evaluating not only my teaching but also myself as a person. I became afraid of showing my lesson plans beforehand because of the criticism I'd receive. I have sat in the department room with my mentor for hours doing work and no word has been spoken between us. All I wanted (and I think every trainee wants) is someone to learn from and help remind them that they are people as well as teachers.

I hoped for some real, critical feedback on my teaching, planning and assessment. I had previously received feedback in the form of the statement, 'The children seem to enjoy it', repeated with gentle regularity. I was looking for something more, though I didn't know what.

I needed someone to shake me out of my role as worksheet administrator and make me realise that I could and must do more than this. Receiving feedback that is neither negative nor positive makes you feel that you are training yourself. What I got was a mentor who believed in active learning methods and self-evaluation, to the extent that she used these methods to encourage me to reflect on my own practice. For example, I was sat down with a lesson graph and two coloured pencils and told to draw a line indicating pupils' levels of productivity and to then mark the points at which I was intervening in their learning. This was a pivotal moment in my teaching.

I really enjoyed being given freedom and space to take risks in lessons. You gave awesome feedback in a supportive manner, which never belittled me. Your advice was amazing because you gave a little advice to work for each week rather than loads of advice that was unachievable.

Thanks for leaving me to my own devices and not mollycoddling me. Your main piece of advice when I got too stressed was invaluable – 'You may be doing this for thirty years. What is the point of burning yourself out now?'.

I would like to tell you how important our mentor meetings were as they gave me the chance to address my worries and seek advice, which I greatly needed. You have stood by me. I would like also to tell you that I wish you had been more straightforward with me. I spent months wondering what you really thought and how I should improve. Despite your observations, you reserved your true opinion so I was unable to change as quickly as I could have.

The amount of help and information that you offered was impeccable. When you combined this with your ability to give me a 'kick up the backside' when necessary, I found my abilities and confidence increasing tremendously.

You always seem to know exactly what to say to raise my spirits and urge me to continue. You never say anything negative about my planning and teaching. You have a knack of making me see where problems may occur without making me feel stupid or incapable.

I have taught lessons that could be considered a disaster; however, you always focus on what went right within the lessons and offer suggestions to overcome the failures.

I knew that you were busy, but I never felt that I was taking time that was important to you.

One of the things that I have found important and useful is the opportunity to have 'mini-meetings' when necessary. A mentor able to spare those impromptu ten minutes whenever a drama or even a simple question arises is a massive help, as this can reduce your worry immediately rather than leaving you to stew in your own bewilderment. Also, the ability to take any question that is stupid or cringeworthy and answer it seriously is a huge relief, especially in moments of madness!

A mentor who knows she is not perfect and actually asks you for advice especially helps to boost confidence!

Another factor that softens the training experience is being treated as an equal and a colleague – having the ability to chat frankly about work (i.e. have a moan about those dreadful kids) without the fear of being judged.

Please think about allowing your trainee to be in charge.

At some points, I did feel like I was competing with you in the classroom. I was ready to teach and you were almost a naughty child who couldn't be quiet. I understand that you have things to say, but it's daunting when I'm trying to teach. The kids still saw you as the boss, not me; and at times I felt that you were overruling me in front of them. I wanted to teach in my own way, and I never really felt that I could without causing offence. You said that my ideas were great, but then you gave me the written feedbacks from hell. Nevertheless, you helped me in many ways, and you made time for me. I feel that I learned a lot from you.

Please don't pour scorn on 'new' methods or on my training course. It's confusing and demoralising when this happens.

From the first day, you made me feel like an asset, rather than a liability.

Our meetings remained focused right to the end. For the first time, I was able to see myself improving. The pupils' work moved from good to outstanding. Sometimes I pretended I was fine with the pressure. Sometimes I worried until the early mornings. Sometimes I lied when I said I was coping. Every time, you were able to see through that and provide me with the praise and motivation to keep going.

I do feel that a graduated introduction to some of my more challenging classes would have been less harrowing at the start of my placement.

Most importantly, you always forced me to focus on the positives in my lessons.

At first, the approach of evaluating each lesson from the standpoint of 'Have the children left the classroom with new knowledge?' was slightly scary. But using this judgement resulted in a whole learning line, which I will always use to reflect on my teaching.

Thank you for your help. I have benefited hugely from the experience. When you have a student teacher again, I have a few tips for you. Try to ensure that you allocate time for regular meetings. I needed more of these, maybe just for peace of mind. Also, I was very touched to have such positive observation sheets, but I needed to know more how to develop my teaching.

Your organisation and professionalism meant that my placement was structured. You were never too busy to help me.

From the start, your comment, 'If you don't feel you can teach, even two minutes before the lesson, then tell me and I'll do it' took so much pressure off. While I would never have done that, the fact that you had said it made me feel so much more confident. You were so straightforward and you said what you thought. This openness and honesty helped me address issues in my own teaching and also meant that your positive comments were sincere.

I watched my mentors enviously and prayed they would reveal the secrets of their success. For the most part, they did. I received great advice about behaviour management, chunking activities, the importance of keeping to the learning objectives and explaining to pupils what their learning will look like.

Schemes of work. Please give them to your trainees!

Be honest with your trainees. If they are not achieving the high expectations you have of them, tell them! Let them know what they are not doing and devise strategies together about how they can rectify this. Do this sooner rather than later! . . . I felt upset and bewildered that no one had sat me down and discussed my shortcomings explicitly and helped me to identify how to put things right.

Initially, I expected a mentor to be someone who would take control of my development and ensure I was on the road to success. How different the process was for me – in a positive way. For me, a successful mentor helps you to develop with strategies for improvement but also allows you to make your own mistakes. My mentor had very high expectations, which helped me seek the best in myself. She gave me ideas and strategies, but only after I had tried alternatives. The idea that I was challenged was a big step in me thinking independently, like a qualified teacher. For example, I had a Year 10 class who were of high ability and were constantly challenging me. Rather than giving me a way forward, she actually challenged me to develop a strategy and implement it. The balance between being supportive and stretching the trainee must be a difficult one, and I was lucky in having both attributes in my mentor.

Commentary

These accounts speak for themselves, but themes do emerge when they are assembled, and these can certainly produce some worthwhile concluding thoughts. For one thing, as we've already said, there is the intensity. The mentoring relationship, it appears, is rarely a bland or indifferent one. Your trainee may well be experiencing it at quite a different level to you. You are dealing with an adult undergoing professional training, but *she* may be dealing with deep, emotional conflicts. Clearly, trainees appreciate it greatly when mentors are able to recognise this.

It's clear, too, that (as we said in Chapter 1) trainees struggle to integrate the huge range of attitudes and practices that surround them, and they look to mentors to support them in this. Teachers who have no interest in innovation shouldn't be mentoring, because trainees need to work with people who will show some creative sympathy for new approaches that may be coming out of university providers. It's easy to be cynical about novelty, but perhaps we need to be considering why we are so wary of it.

There are other interesting patterns. In another book (*How to be a Brilliant Teacher*), I have suggested that excellent practice may occur when teachers resolve paradoxes or reconcile apparent opposites. For example, brilliant teaching may need to be both creative and structured, both premeditated and spontaneous, both expert and interactive. It seems from these trainee accounts that excellent mentoring often similarly deals with contradictions.

For example, there is the issue of freedom and direction. Trainees praise mentors who give them freedom, who let them make their own mistakes, who don't overrule them in the classroom. On the other hand, they are distressed by mentors who ignore them, or whose expectations of independence are too high. Finding a dynamic balance between these approaches depends upon clarity, flexibility and sensitivity.

A question that arises often in this connection is that of leaving the trainee alone with classes. This may seem a pragmatic, even trivial, issue, but it's actually emblematic of attitudes surrounding the training relationship. Some mentors will never allow their trainees to be left alone to teach. Some are even of the view that this is illegal or unethical – which, apart from some health-and-safety considerations relevant to specific subjects and activities, is untrue. On the other hand, some mentors will desert the trainee at the earliest possible opportunity. These are matters of trust, confidence and negotiation and, of course, depend upon the status and competence of the trainee at any given time. She is, after all, working towards independence.

There are other attitudinal paradoxes. Obviously, trainees like to be praised. They like to be told about things they've done well. They like to feel valued and accepted. As teachers, we know very well how important self-esteem is to progress. On the other hand, trainees clearly want to be told how to develop. They want critiques that are challenging without being negative. It's worth remembering one of the comments quoted above from a trainee with an over-relaxed mentor: 'Receiving feedback which is neither negative nor positive makes you feel that you are training yourself.'

In fact, trainees clearly have felt cheated when doubts about their progress have not been shared, or have been shared too late. We commented on this in Chapter 2. The inclination for the mentor to keep quiet, for fear of upsetting trainee confidence, must be modulated with the need (and, arguably, the right) of the trainee to know what's wrong so that he can do something about it. While trainees dislike unrelieved negativity, they certainly don't appreciate insincere or misleading flattery.

Another paradox that emerges is what we might loosely call the mentor/coach paradox. The mentor needs to be an expert, a figure whom the trainee respects and learns from, but she needs to be human as well. One trainee comments on how the relationship strengthens when the mentor asks the trainee for advice. It might be worth considering when you last did this. After all, trainees probably know more about some professional issues than you do. Unlike you, they have time (on most training programmes) to read and discuss; they are receiving training in new methods and new content. Making use of this in your school will be of positive benefit to all concerned.

Expertise, in fact, may seem at times to be a necessary evil. You need to be a good teacher to be a mentor, but you must moderate your expertise so that the trainee isn't intimidated by it. It's a given that you're better at teaching than he is – it would be odd and disturbing if you weren't – but you must work to ensure that this of itself doesn't create a barrier between you. You may need to work explicitly at remembering what it's like to find the work difficult, and the early stages that you had to pass through to become the expert that you are.

Stress and the trainee teacher

Pressure is a fact of life for trainees. Virtually every trainee feels that the training experience is the hardest thing he's ever done. I have trained nurses, businessmen and, in one case, a murder-squad detective inspector, who all agreed with this. Dealing with stress for trainees is another creative paradox. You want them to experience the pressures of the job: if they appear carefree, then something is probably wrong, but you don't want them to succumb entirely.

Training is stressful; you can't change that. Of course, you can help trainees with coping strategies. For example, you can encourage them to map out weekly templates, which include fixed marking, preparation, relaxing and drinking times. You can advise on staggering the workload and on sharing the planning burden. Even more potently, though, you can intervene in the vicious stress circle in which many trainees find themselves.

This cycle is based on the false notion that the trainee shouldn't be feeling the stress that she's feeling. She feels guilty about the stress. She is aware that (probably) she is not carrying a full teacher's workload. She perhaps doesn't have final responsibility for any pupils; she probably isn't teaching a full timetable; she may not be carrying out voluntary supervisions; she may not be running clubs or teams; she may have few pastoral duties. Nevertheless, she feels overwhelmed – not only suicidally stressed by her workload, but depressed because, as far as she can see, things can only get worse. If it's this bad now, what's it going to be like in the future?

There are two stages in lifting a trainee out of this cyclical panic. The first is to point out that it's perfectly reasonable for her to feel stressed. She is doing a new and difficult job in an alien and sometimes hostile environment. She is working systems she didn't create and only partly understands. She is making and trying to service many new and potentially threatening relationships with adults and children. She is potentially being assessed at every moment. She has to do things – plan formally, write assignments, research and reflect on evidence – that trained teachers don't have to do. So, she should stop feeling guilty about being stressed. If she weren't stressed, then that would be something to worry about.

Second, you can demolish the fear that things can only get worse. The point here is that many of the activities that a trainee is involved in will, as the training progresses, diminish spectacularly in size. We said in Chapter 1 that a new trainee may spend many hours preparing a twenty-minute lesson activity. She will craft it, worry, scrap it, recraft it, seek help with it, give it up and start again. Within a few weeks or months, this polarity will have reversed, and a week's lessons will take an hour to plan. This vanishing workload pressure is often dramatic and swift, and, especially in the early stages, trainees have to be reassured, and to trust, that this will happen. Contact with someone recently trained may help to convince your trainee that things will get better. She may be stressed by the work, but she shouldn't be stressed about the stress.

This book is based on the views and experiences of mentors, tutors and trainees. It intends to stimulate, to counsel, to structure and to solve problems. In this respect, we hope, it plays the role of mentor.

Suggested reading

Various individual chapters are followed by references for further reading. The following texts may also be of interest:

Arthur, J., Davison, J. and Moss, J. (1997) *Subject mentoring in secondary school*, London: Routledge.

Fletcher, S. (2000) *Mentoring in schools: a handbook of good practice*, London: Routledge.

Garvey, B., Langridge, K. and Hailstone, P. (2003) *Mentoring in schools pocketbook*, London: Management Pocketbooks.

Newell, S. and Jeffery, D. (2002) *Behaviour management in the classroom: a transactional analysis approach*, London: David Fulton.

Wright, T. (2007) *How to be a brilliant trainee teacher*, London: Routledge.

Wright, T. (2008) *How to be a brilliant teacher*, London: Routledge.

Index

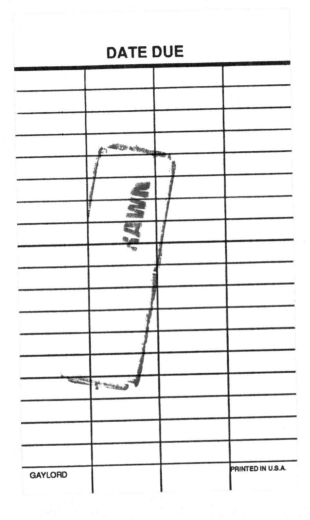